Retailing Logistics
& Fresh Food Packaging

Retailing Logistics
& Fresh Food Packaging

Managing Change in the Supply Chain

Kerstin Gustafsson, Gunilla Jönson,
David Smith & Leigh Sparks

The Chartered Institute of
Logistics and Transport (UK)

KOGAN
PAGE

London and Philadelphia

First published in Great Britain and the United States in 2006 by Kogan Page Limited

120 Pentonville Road
London N1 9JN
United Kingdom
www.kogan-page.co.uk

525 South 4th Street, #241
Philadelphia PA 19147
USA

© Kerstin Gustafsson, Gunilla Jönson, David Smith and Leigh Sparks, 2006

ISBN 0 7494 4645 5

British Library Cataloguing-in-Publication Data

A CIP record for this book is available from the British Library.

Library of Congress Cataloging-in-Publication Data

Retailing logistics and fresh food packaging : managing change in the supply chain / Kerstin Gustafsson ... [et al.].
    p. cm.
Includes bibliographical references.
ISBN 0-7494-4645-5
    1. Produce trade–Management. 2. Farm produce–Packaging. 3. Business logistics–Management. 4. Retail trade–Management. I. Gustafsson, Kerstin, 1956– . II. Title.
HD9000.5.R38 2006
381'.410685–dc22   2006008270

Typeset by Saxon Graphics Ltd, Derby
Printed and bound in the United States by Thomson-Shore, Inc.

Contents

Preface

We rely on fresh food to live. Its quality and freshness have a direct effect on our health and diet. Food retailers compete strongly in the area of fresh food as well as in a myriad of other products. Consumers want to see the best products on display at appropriate prices so they can identify value in the retail food offer. For retailers, making sure the stores and shelves are stocked is a fundamental component of modern retailing. This fact has increasingly compelled retailers to think about how they structure, control and amend supply chains to ensure they are effective and efficient. With changes in production, logistics, retailing and consumer tastes, combined with increasingly technological capabilities and global sourcing reach, this task has become ever more complex. More and more difficult choices have to be made. How can the organizations involved in supply chains make sense of the sometimes conflicting tensions and pressures? What are the 'right' decisions and appropriate solutions?

This book has its origins in research work being undertaken for higher degrees by two of the authors from two different countries. From an initial meeting at a seminar, a series of discussions and conversations have taken place, broadened to include the research supervisors. From different perspectives and backgrounds, a common cause has been identified. The concept of packaging logistics embodies this set of beliefs about the future of the food retail supply chain. The search for a reduction in complexity and an increase in common handling systems has marked out this field, often in the form of a variety of returnable transit or retailing packaging units. Such a view is at the heart of this book.

This volume identifies the changes occurring in fresh food retail supply chains through the lens of packaging logistics. It tries to support organizations in developing their understanding of the changes and opportunities involved. We hope that academics and business managers will find useful elements here. One thing is certain: the pressure to get retail supply chains 'right' throughout the supply chain is not going to diminish. Packaging logistics is one way of cutting through what needs to be done.

Kerstin Gustafsson, Gunilla Jönson, David Smith and Leigh Sparks

1

Packaging Logistics and Fresh Food Retailing: An Introduction

It cannot escape even the casual consumer's notice that the way in which fresh food is sold has changed. It is fair to say that there has been a transformation of fresh food retailing. This is evident across Europe, both in the changing formats of food retailing and in the way in which fresh food is presented and retailed within the shop system. Dramatic transformations of the retail structure in many countries have also altered the supply system, as retailers have gained power and control from manufacturers, producers and wholesalers. Some logistics changes have been driven by legal requirements on the safe and healthy handling and supply of food products. Others come about from alterations to consumer demands and requirements and the development of new products and new product categories by manufacturers and retailers.

Substantial change has also been aided by a realization that supply chains, particularly in fresh food, can be simplified and reorganized so as to become more efficient and effective. In particular the scope for improvements in packaging logistics to produce better solutions for timely and appropriate handling and supply has been considerable. The packaging, handling and movement of products has become of vital concern for retailers and suppliers, including producers, manufacturers, logistics services providers and of course handling system suppliers. These concerns and the implications of the solutions are felt from the point of production through the supply chain to the point of purchase and even consumption.

This chapter introduces the three key themes of this book: retail logistics, packaging and change management. We use these three themes as exploratory tools to help readers consider the 'why and how' behind the development of high-quality handling systems for transporting fresh food along temperature controlled supply chains from producer to retail store. We take each theme in turn and set out some of the general challenges businesses face in finding appropriate solutions in the area of fresh food retailing and packaging logistics. The aim in this chapter is to outline our approach to the subjects, lay out the structure of this book and suggest how this book could assist businesses and students alike.

LOGISTICS: WHY BOTHER WITH WHAT GOES ON BEHIND THE SCENES?

It is quite natural, even in today's business environment, to believe that it is only production or selling that matters in a successful business plan. The emphasis is often on manufacturing or retailing. How the product actually makes the journey from producer to consumer is of increasing concern, though attention still lags behind the consideration given to producing and selling. This goes hand in hand with a belief that what goes on 'behind the scenes' does not really matter to the success of a business and certainly does not justify major business resource or thought from the top of the company. Whilst this is now changing, and logistics directors and executives are more commonly found, logistics and supply chain management have for too many, for too long, been an afterthought.

Many companies and organizations believe that it is quite sufficient to let logistics proceed with a lower level of management attention or, better still, simply to outsource the activity to a third party or business partner with no further management time spent on its control or development. Such views are misguided in that the logistics and supply functions represent real opportunities to enhance business and supply chain performance. The problems of supplying often volatile consumer demand are substantial. The costs of getting it wrong can be considerable, both in the short and in the long term. Management time and attention on supply chain activities, whether carried out in-house or outsourced, can provide considerable benefits.

Whilst some companies certainly continue to survive with an outdated business philosophy of downplaying supply systems, it is our conviction that those companies that are most successful actually pay a great deal of attention to improving, enhancing and developing those activities that go on 'behind the scenes'. In the long run such attention to detail provides a winning advantage on service and costs. Getting logistics right can provide substantial cost savings and service gains. This has become particularly evident in the area of fresh food, with the emphasis on freshness, quality and timeliness, but at low cost.

Centres of excellence and hidden heroes

Such activities as supply chain management, logistics, packaging and change management have proven to be critical success factors for well-known companies. As is often the case, it is worth a look at what makes this vision increase the success of an enterprise. It is worth asking the question: why do some of the top companies develop levels of excellence within their 'back-room' operations – operations that seem to be outside their core business and not visible to the outside world? For example, why are many of the best retailers (eg Wal-Mart) also excellent at the management of their supply chain, logistics and packaging? Why, for instance, do such companies believe that their ability to expand into new formats and forms of retailing (eg Tesco.com) is possible only because they have developed centres of excellence in the support functions of supply chain, logistics and packaging? The simple answer might be that such retailers are simply adopting good practice in all areas of their activities. However, it would seem that in fact these leading retailers (and selected partners) have recognized that the supply chain is a potential source of competitive advantage and have chosen to manage it accordingly.

The evidence for such an assertion is often visible only to those who, in addition to having access to allow them to look behind the scenes, also possess the know-how to identify the critical success factors that exist in those operations. These success factors have been developed by knowledgeable operators who strive continuously to improve their operations, their systems, their productivity and their service. Success is found both in the strategic direction set and in the many points of operational detail that need to be managed by supply chain practitioners.

In many ways this book is about their story. Supply chain operatives are in some ways the hidden heroes of retailing, manufacturing and logistics. This is an opportunity to bring them and their ideas into the spotlight. It is an opportunity to tell what they have to say about what they do and how they do it. To many, this should be a story well worth telling. It should be appreciated even by expert practitioners, as much improvement potential remains. It will also potentially be of much benefit to businesses in developing nations where improving the efficiency, effectiveness and safety of food supply and retail systems has become an urgent necessity, for environmental, health and competitive reasons. To some, this story will be a challenge or even a threat. We hope, however, to help businesses to continue to move forward by providing them with a structure that they can use for their own analysis, together with some tools for effecting different implementation strategies to suit their business objectives. By focusing on packaging logistics in fresh food retailing we aim to illustrate how businesses can be enhanced and assisted through thinking about key changes in core and support activities.

PACKAGING: HOW AM I SUPPOSED TO KNOW THERE IS A MISSING LINK?

One objective of this book, and the reason it is focused on packaging logistics, is to provoke people into thinking differently about logistics and packaging and to help them think of these business disciplines from different perspectives. These perspectives are based on real business experiences, including all the challenges and opportunities that form the complexity of the business world today. It is hoped that, by our raising of packaging and logistics issues and use of different approaches and case studies, the packaging and logistics industry will be able to apply the most appropriate models to help them serve their customers more profitably into the future.

The functions of packaging have been well known for some time, but focusing on the functions alone tends to provide a narrow and segmented view of the potential for packaging in logistics. By taking a wider perspective, the ideas behind packaging logistics can be explored and demonstrated. Packaging logistics takes a supply chain approach to the development of packaging, seeking efficiency and effectiveness across supply chains by the coordinated development of packaging activities and solutions. The need for a supply chain approach suggests a requirement for coordination and change in logistics, including packaging, systems.

In this book, we point out the importance of taking into account the components in supply that are often forgotten when designing a new packaging system. How do we make sure that all parties involved in a development process have the same level and application of professional knowledge? How do we include the experiences from those groups of people involved in the supply chain that are visible to only one business? It is our conviction that this process is often about seeking ways of communication amongst all parts of the supply chain, in order to create a meeting of minds where good operational ideas can be exchanged and then used in the creation of a full list of requirements for any new packaging logistics system.

This is important as it is often forgotten that a new packaging system influences or, even worse, interferes with or impedes other systems along the supply chain. A good example of how things change is to take the traditional packaging design process that starts with the manufacturer's view of the supply chain. For example, the manufacturer's understanding might be that the business needs to deliver its products on full pallets to all its customers. But, as the structure and nature of the retail supply system has changed, so the need to send the full pallet direct to the end customer is also changing. This raises the question: how does the manufacturer learn about these changes and, more importantly, how can it know in what ways it should be changing its packaging specification to suit the new demands of its customer's customer and, at the same time, continue to maintain or improve its profitability? As the supply chain ethos has developed, so the interactions along the chain have become more important, and it is no longer sensible or possible to manage supply systems as non-connected transactional entities.

Amongst the aims of this book therefore are the needs to understand the potential of packaging logistics and to help readers identify 'blind spots' and explain how to deal with them. What inputs are needed when formulating a specification at the point where the packaging design decision is being made? How can we learn about and assess the uses in the supply chain both upstream and downstream of our own involvement in the logistics process? Could a new packaging system be even more profitable if suppliers, customers and even the customer's customer were more fully involved? How can we ensure that modern environmental concerns are fully embraced by all? What scope is there in packaging logistics to introduce and use appropriate technologies, whether the technology is a returnable packaging system or the use of radio frequency identification (RFiD)?

For too long, packaging has been assumed to be a relatively lower-order decision. Our position and analysis here are that decisions about packaging in the broadest sense can help integrate and enhance supply chains. Nowhere is this better illustrated than in packaging logistics in fresh food retailing, where the entire supply chain has been altered, yet scope remains for considerable further advances.

CHANGE MANAGEMENT: LIFE IS TOO BUSY TO WASTE TIME THINKING!

One of the implications of taking a packaging logistics approach is that it cuts across traditional, functional and organizational boundaries and management. As such its implication is essentially about change management. In most situations this change management has to operate at the same time as existing systems have to continue to deliver. This makes it enormously challenging, and in some cases threatening, both within the organization and outside the organization's boundaries as new partnerships and processes are developed.

Few managers or businesses are ever able to make truly holistic business decisions that take into account every cost and benefit consideration across the full range of possible implications. This may be seen by some as an ideal way of doing things, but in reality we all have to live with 'good enough' decisions based on selecting the most important business criteria that we believe will influence the success or failure of a product, a project or an endeavour and implementing decisions quickly. We also know that many of the decisions we make are as much influenced by our intuition and instinct for what is right for the business as they are by rigorously logical thinking and analysis. We also know that sometimes our intuition is based on deeper emotions and reactions that we use to guard our business interests, often based on earlier experiences of success and failure. But, whatever the quality of our decisions, we all have a natural desire to improve and enhance our ability to achieve success and avoid failure. Sometimes, however, it may not look like that.

Selecting quickly only that information that is relevant for appropriate decision making

One of the aims of this book is to accept that this 'ordinary' type of decision-making process is normal. We aim to assist and help those readers who wish to move forward, not only in a general way but also in more specific directions, if they are involved or interested in the logistics and packaging industry and its implications for change. This industry, like so many, continues to evolve, change and develop amid complex and turbulent business and competitive pressures. Change is an everyday occurrence in this sector, and new systems often require considerable alterations to existing practices.

So what information do we really need for our decisions? What information needs to be gathered that is critical without being trivial, rigorous without being simplistic, and effective without being indecisive? Why do we get so many different results from what appear to be similar situations? Here our task is not to take on the whole of business management theory. Our task is to set the scene and so guide the thought processes of readers quickly through the broad sweep of possibilities, so that they can then focus more closely on the challenges facing the packaging and logistics industry and their own business situations.

Using case studies as an intelligent tool for good–quality decisions

Most business decisions are based in some part on existing practices, either internal to the firm or else understood to be succeeding elsewhere. Decisions are often based on comparisons and analogues in other companies, supply chains and countries. There is a danger in this of a degree of 'group-think' or at least narrowness of vision. Are the comparisons appropriate? Has the wrong core model been selected? Were there enough different core models provided to encourage thought and development of new ideas and appropriate solutions? What actually provides the competitive benefit or advantage?

We use a considerable number of case studies and case illustrations in this book. We hope to demonstrate clearly why certain case studies were chosen, with a full appreciation of the business position that they represent. Different case studies are put forward to represent contrasting business conditions. We aim to demonstrate that an understanding of why these particular case studies were selected, as well as what they tell us, will help readers choose the appropriate cases and issues to apply to their own business challenges. The cases are not necessarily exemplars, but are designed to provoke thought about current practices and behaviours.

It is our belief that, when presented with real-life business challenges, it is worth taking the time to think first about which case model or example to follow. We will present clear theoretical reasons why readers should choose one model rather than another to suit the business circumstances in which a company may find itself. For example, is a company's future growth about continuing business as usual or is it being faced with a situation where it really needs to leapfrog from its current position and take a radically different place in its market, with its competitors and their products? Alternatively, a company may have just completed such a radical repositioning, or acquisition or merger, and be in the throes and turmoil of adjusting to the strange new conditions in which it finds itself. The circumstances will demand different solutions or practices.

Some of these new circumstances may feel very strange and uncomfortable to those involved. Managers may wish to return to the comfort of the best of the earlier ways and structure of working. Or they may be trying to be brave and courageous to make the best of the new situation. Whichever it is, we have identified a need to help those involved in various companies in a range of such different circumstances. Our discussion and cases should help in a variety of such situations where issues of packaging logistics are emerging and where operations and change are no longer neatly confined to internal business functions, areas or 'silos' but instead transcend functional and business boundaries.

How to handle unexpected and unforeseen reactions

This need, in our view, is about the ability to step back for a moment from the full thrust of the endeavour and select the right type of model for that particular situation. We believe that, to make that selection properly, we need to have a grasp of what makes one model more suitable than another for a specific business condition. This appears to be straightforward and common sense, most of the time, especially when we have the time to think and reflect. But often, in the heat of competitive pressure and the threat of new entrants into our marketplace, it is a totally natural instinct to jump straight in, to protect our business interests and position, to throw up barriers both commercial and political, to fight vigorously for our corner, and to hurl accusations and even abuse at our competitors and potential collaborators and so undermine their position.

All this is understandable and happens frequently as we see all around us, not only in business but also in many walks of life. But what if the chosen strategy is not the best strategy for other groups on whom we are dependent or for whom we are there to provide a service? What then? How do we step back and review our decisions? How do we start to think through the impact on those outside our immediate focus? What tools can we use to pause for thought? What can we bring quickly to the debate to influence decisions so that the outcome is better not worse? And better or worse for whom? Ourselves in the short term? Our customers in the long term? Our product development? Our way of working? Our way of thinking?

We all know that there is one thing we cannot avoid: it is that business change is taking place, and often at a rapid pace. Such change can be confusing and overwhelming and affects many business partners. We know that we cannot be like the ostrich and bury our head in the sand. We know that, no matter how comfortable it may feel to continue doing things the way we like doing them, we often have to face up to the discomfort of discarding comfortable conditions, move out of our comfort zone and venture into new, unknown, uncharted circumstances. As competition increases, often on a global or international basis rather than just on a national stage, and certainly at a supply chain level as opposed to a functional level, so the pressures will increase.

On the other hand, many people enjoy change, they enjoy a challenge and they thrive on discovering new ideas, new products, new markets, new ways of serving customers and new ways of growing a business. Such people and businesses embrace change and the scope it provides for new opportunities and methods of working. But change for change's sake also has its own problems.

Applying guidance from a broader perspective

Our objective in this book therefore is to help people in the fresh food retailing, packaging and logistics industries to recognize where they and their company are in their business environment. We aim to help them by putting their situations and challenges into a broader perspective, by offering a selection of models and experiences from which they can choose a business model that is appropriate to them and their circumstances.

At a broad level this is about business change management, about analysis and action and about reflection, review and redirection. But this is not a generalist book about business change. We take management change theory as one of the tools that we use in our analysis, and one that will help decide which case model to select when moving a business forward. But our work is more specific than that, based on the concept of packaging logistics in fresh food retailing and managing the necessary change in the supply systems.

At another broad level this book is also about such issues as confidence, attitudes, responses in traumatic experiences, courage, pessimism and other personality development models. But again this is not a generalist book about personality or about crisis management or trauma therapy. We will refer to these aspects when it is appropriate to do so, where it will help to take that step back in the middle of the rush of the business challenge, in order to reflect if there is a better way forward for the business. Instead, the book takes fresh food retailing and packaging logistics, examines the changes under way and considers how businesses could best react to them.

THE STRUCTURE OF THE BOOK

In this introduction we have raised some questions around each of the three themes of this book: retail logistics, packaging and change management. These themes are explored through the various chapters and cases. The approach is to explain the topics and then deal with each theme in turn, giving case study examples to help link the theory with practical business situations. Figure 1.1 describes the space in which this book operates. In this figure the theme of retail logistics is disaggregated into retailing and logistics to emphasize the driving force of retail change on logistics change. There are aspects of retail, logistics and packaging change that go on essentially without interactions with other elements of the business. Likewise, however, there are also interactions amongst these three elements. At the centre of these interactions is the issue of change management in packaging logistics. These interactions are critical given the dimensions of change and opportunity and the speed of change present in such supply chains. Managing this process is the heart of this book.

The object of this book is fresh food. The supply system for fresh food has been transformed in recent years both through retail change and through changes in the location and nature of production.

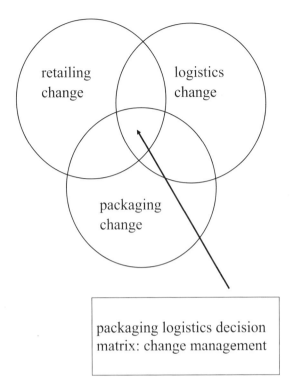

Figure 1.1   *Packaging logistics, retailing and change management*

However, the supply system has also undergone a packaging logistics revolution in some situations, as a search for efficiency and effectiveness has altered relationships, processes and activities. The more widespread use of returnable plastic packaging is one element of these changes and is at the heart of this book. How did such changes come about? How can the change process be structured and managed? How can retailing, packaging and logistics changes be integrated in a modern supply system?

As is outlined below, the next four chapters take the three elements of retailing, logistics and packaging in fresh food in turn (Chapters 2 to 4), followed by the interactions amongst all three (Chapter 5). Major case studies (Chapter 6) are then used to illustrate and explore the choices available, supported by a selection of smaller application case studies (Chapter 7). The final two chapters (Chapters 8 and 9) provide lessons and conclusions and discuss some issues for the future. Figure 1.2 shows this structure. Further details of these chapters are provided below.

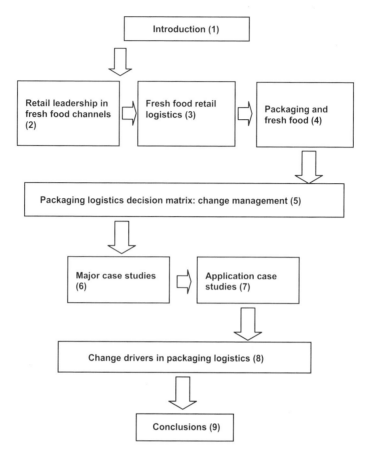

Figure 1.2   *Organization of this book*

Chapter 2: Retail leadership in fresh food channels

The first element explored in some detail is retailing change. The chapter provides an analysis of the powerful drivers of change and development that have been taking place in food retailing in the UK and Europe. The chapter then discusses the concept of leadership in fresh food channels, where the retailer is identified as the channel leader setting the pace and managing channel change and restructuring.

Chapter 3: Fresh food retail logistics

The second element is the consideration of logistics change in fresh food retailing. In particular the chapter focuses on the role of logistics as one of the enablers delivering the marketing promise to consumers. From this broad base, the chapter focuses on the characteristics of temperature controlled supply chains, which are critical to the success and growth of the fresh food retail market.

Chapter 4: Packaging and fresh food

The third element explored is that of fresh food packaging. The chapter begins with a broad outline of the key components and drivers of change in packaging development. Within this broad background the chapter compares and contrasts the packaging debate about the benefits of using corrugated packaging and of using plastic crates. This debate reflects issues of environmental concern, supply chain productivity and also product protection, especially over the extended distances of global sourcing. This theme is of growing importance to operators, especially those who are seeking to change their methods in line with the industry leaders. The chapter cites recent research from Sweden, focusing on the issue of temperature integrity along the supply chain, which is going to be a key driver of development over the next five years.

Chapter 5: Packaging logistics decision matrix: change management

The interactions amongst retailing, logistics and packaging change are explored though a model of the packaging logistics decision matrix, which enables readers to position themselves and companies within a broader theoretical framework. The chapter focuses on recent research into the issues in the packaging industry in general and more particularly in the arena of fresh food packaging. This packaging decision matrix provides a mechanism for business choice and decision making. A particular emphasis is placed on the need to manage change throughout a supply chain.

Chapter 6: Major case studies

The earlier chapters have set the scene for this chapter, which presents two major model case studies, taken from the UK and Sweden. The first model case study is of a large UK food retailer, detailing the dynamics of its rapid implementation of its second-generation plastic trays for fresh foods. The second model case study is of a large retailing and supplier association in Sweden, detailing the dynamics of its implementation of a packaging strategy for fresh foods. The chapter provides the detail of the model case studies before drawing out some of the issues and implications, focusing on the three themes outlined in the earlier chapters. More importantly, it suggests criteria to apply in selecting an approach to follow in a particular industry setting.

Chapter 7: Application case studies

Having presented contrasting model case studies in the previous chapter, the book now moves on to provide a broader range of smaller, more focused application case studies. The objective is to provide readers, from within this selection, with something that relates closely to their own business situations, and then to demonstrate the advantages and disadvantages of applying the different model case studies to their own businesses. As well as gaining a broad understanding of the retail and packaging industries, together with a greater knowledge of the issues of change management, managers and businesses can move on to a practical review for themselves.

Chapter 8: Change drivers in packaging logistics

By this stage in the book, it is possible to step back and provide some analysis of how the drivers of change influence fresh food packaging and packaging logistics implementation as a whole. Here we take a holistic view of the distinctive components of this book: retailing logistics, fresh food packaging, and the challenge of change management across the three topics. The analysis briefly compares and contrasts the theoretical assumptions of this book with the practical lessons from the analysis. Its main aim, however, is to provide a set of practical guides or questions to help operators evaluate their position.

Chapter 9: Conclusions

This final chapter draws out the implications of the previous analysis both for industry and for the academic study of the area. It identifies gaps in our knowledge and recommends areas for additional research and practical help, particularly in the light of increasing legislation surrounding temperature controlled food supply chains. A concluding section on possible future issues and their implications is included.

SUMMARY

This book has been written so that it will be of interest not only to the professional, already working in this field, but also to those who want a general understanding of the issues that are important in making a success of packaging logistics and its implementation. It draws on academic material and practical case studies to examine this vital and fast-changing area. It is hoped that academics and practitioners will find it helpful.

Our overall aim is to help businesses and industry in a practical way. We achieve this by using and analysing case studies. The book should be of value to plastic and corrugated packaging suppliers, manufacturers, retailers, logistics service providers, their trade associations, and those preparing academic or executive development courses or specialist academic research as a source of case study material for retail, logistics, packaging, supply chain, and industrial or business change management.

2 Retail Leadership in Fresh Food Channels

Retailing is a huge part of many economies. Within the retail sector, food retailing is the largest and most important component. Perhaps 25 per cent of all enterprises in the European Union (EU) are involved in retailing. About 12 per cent of the total working population are engaged in retailing. There are well over 3.5 million shops in the EU. Food retailing makes up perhaps 40 per cent of the total in many countries. The retail sector is enormous and influential. Within these totals, however, are massive contrasts (Dawson, 1995). There are many single-shop businesses, but there are also some of the largest companies in Europe. There are large and small fixed shops, mobile shops and now even virtual shops. Retailing is a local affair with local demands: but Euro-brands are increasing and indeed global brands are important. Retail sales are increasing but the number of shops is falling and their format is changing. Low pay characterizes much of the sector, but managerial pay is above average and for the most successful executives rewards are considerable. Retailing is a business sector of contrasts, undergoing considerable change.

One of the fundamental components of this change has occurred in the supply of products to retailers. Nowhere is this more apparent than in food retailing. The nature, practice and control of supply channels have all been adjusted in the search for efficiencies and effectiveness suitable to meet the demands of modern retailers and consumers. This chapter aims to consider the nature and direction of change in food retailing and thus set the scene for further analysis of logistic and packaging changes in fresh food supply systems. Throughout the chapter, issues of leadership in channels and the ways in which retailers can control and reconstruct fresh food channels are recognized. The next chapter then focuses specifically on the way in which retail change affects the practice of logistics in fresh food channels.

Retailing is traditionally defined as the sale of articles, either individually or in small numbers, directly to the consumer. Whilst this might sound straightforward, it is but a simplistic statement about a complex set of processes and relationships. This chapter takes the key components of the process of retailing (see Table 2.1) and illustrates the distinctive and changing nature of the food retail sector and some of the issues this raises for fresh food supply channels.

CULTURE AND RETAIL CONSUMERS

Any consideration of retailing has to begin with the country or local environments in which retailing takes place. Retailing must be responsive to the culture within which it operates. These cultural norms are derived from societal and economic situations. Retailing is an economic transaction, but also in many cases it is also a social interaction. The norms of economic and social behaviour permeate, inform and, on occasion, constrain the retail operations. The restrictive shop opening hours in much of Germany are a legal recognition of cultural dimensions to the organization of society, and have long-standing roots. The restriction of alcohol sales to government-owned shops in Sweden or parts of Canada reflects societal concerns. The persistence of fresh produce markets in Mediterranean Europe and much of Asia derives from traditional patterns of food preparation and consumption.

For retailers, there are a number of implications of culture and its component aspects. First, as culture is absorbed, learnt and transmitted from generation to generation, certain aspects of culture may become deep-rooted and thus hard to change. There are therefore boundaries to what can be sold or how or when it can be sold. What is acceptable

Table 2.1   The retailing process

Components	Key Topics	Issues in Food Retailing	Implications for Fresh Food Channels
Culture and Retail Consumers	Local vs global culture. Cultural stability. Demographics. Consumer behaviour.	Food culture(s). Local population aspects. Sizes of households. Food lifestyles. Convenience and the use of time.	Need for availability to be high and products to be packaged or available in varying sizes. Greater mix of products and quality.
Retail Locations and Outlets	Decentralization. Polarization of scale.	Development of superstores. 'Food deserts'. Smaller stores at key travel points. Convenience focus.	Volume of distribution requirements to superstores and difficulty of delivery in some urban and rural locations.
Shopkeepers and Retail Managers	Organizational power. Centralized management. Management skills and capabilities.	Central control of standards. Store management skills and qualities.	Quality control at shop level and professionalism at buyer and distributor levels.
Product Sourcing and Distribution	Technology use. International sourcing. Logistics and supply chain management. Branding.	Control of supply – absolute and quality. Management of the supply chain and protection against hazards. Availability. Standard handling systems. Maintenance of brand value.	Efficiency, effectiveness and quality in fresh food channels over a wider supply base.
Business Relationships	Supply chain management. Finance. Outsourcing and partnerships.	Partnerships in the channel.	Supply system needs to be efficient and effective across the channel from producer to consumer, including intermediaries and service providers.
Merchandising and Selling	Selling skills and techniques. Display systems.	Display quality and skills. Freshness of product.	Requirement for presentation to be assisted by the packaging systems and for supply to provide a quality product for display.

within societies varies, as a visit to any traditional 'wet market' in Asia quickly demonstrates. Secondly, a shared culture binds some groups together and thus can provide the basis for identifying markets or market segments. We might, for example, point to the presence of immigrant communities and particular consumer behaviour patterns in large cities across the world. Thirdly, however, we have to be careful not to overemphasize the responsive nature of retailing. Whilst retailing operates mainly within cultural norms and thus reflects these, retailers can also shape these cultural norms in many ways. Retail operations and environments are not neutral entities but rather manufacture, condition and structure consumer moods and behaviours and, over the long term, may influence accepted cultural norms. The success of Western food retailers in a number of Asian countries reflects an ability both to capture and integrate local market and food practices, and to educate and direct consumers to the possible benefits of Western food practices. Exciting hybrid stores containing the best of both worlds, eg Giant hypermarkets in Malaysia, are one outcome of this 'melding' process.

One basic constraint on the development of retailing is the demographic structure of the market. At its most simple, demographic change relates to features such as the number, age structure and location of individuals and households. For retailers, changes in these dimensions are fundamental, as they affect the size and location of their target markets. An examination of some demographic aspects in Europe immediately identifies far-reaching changes in recent decades.

First, whilst growth continues in the number of people in most countries, the rate of growth has reduced substantially over the last half-century. We can attribute this to lower birth rates, fertility levels and socio-economic changes, such as the full participation of women in the paid labour force. For retailers it means that they can no longer rely on previous assumptions of 'natural' population growth to increase market size.

Secondly, whilst the population may (just) still be growing, there has been a fundamental shift in its age composition. The decline in the birth rate, coupled with a reduction in child mortality, longer life expectancy and improved medical care, has resulted in a much more 'elderly' population structure than before. Even though large numbers of this elderly population are more affluent and active than previous generations, retailers still have to consider how they respond to this and other population segments. The retail offer has to be adjusted to meet the changing numbers in different target markets. These different age segments may have very different attitudes.

Thirdly, demographic changes have been allied with socio-economic and lifestyle changes, such as a later age of marriage and higher divorce rates, to restructure radically both the number and the structure of households in most countries. There are far more households now in Europe than before, but there are fewer people (often only one person) in each of them. For retailers, this can provide opportunities and market growth, eg fridges and cookers, but also requires them to adapt their product sizes and ranges, eg introduce food packet sizes suitable for individual consumption.

Consumers are also dynamic (see Marshall 2004). Consumers change and consumer behaviour alters over time. Norms of consumer behaviour that were once thought to be inviolable or immutable have altered considerably. As economies and societies have developed, so consumer desires have changed. What is important to the society or to groups of consumers has evolved. The way in which time and money are interrelated is one illustration of the process. Consumers in many economies use time very differently to previous generations. Consumers and retailers are increasingly involved in a 24/7 economy. Equally, consumers have a different potential for and perception of travel, both generally and for shopping. The implications of this for retailing are fundamental. Consumers' needs, and their ability to satisfy these needs, have altered dramatically, giving rise to retailing concepts such as organic superstores, lifestyle shopping, outlet malls, convenience stores and fast food. At the product level, changing attitudes towards vegetarianism, meat consumption, microwaveable meals or the acceptability of fur or products based on animal testing are equivalent examples. The prevalence or otherwise of fresh food in the diet and attempts to promote material trends in diet and healthy eating also fit into this cultural and lifestyle change.

We can identify a number of implications for retailing from various cultural and consumer changes (see also Bowlby, 2000; Dawson, 1995; Marsden, Flynn and Harrison, 2000; Marshall, 1995; Miller *et al*, 1998; Murcott, 1998).

First, there are trends in *consumption*, ie the general structure of demand and the amount of specific goods consumed. An example is the modern superstore or hypermarket. Here, the increased product ranges in the areas of ready meals and prepared foods reflect changing demand patterns. The segmentation of products by price or by other attributes, eg organic, gluten-free, healthy living or children's meals, is a reaction to wider trends in the market. The extension of food retailers into banking, insurance, health care and also services such as mobile phones and top-up phone cards also illustrates the shift in consumption towards services.

There are then implications for *consumer behaviour*, ie consumer decisions as to which of their wants they wish to satisfy and how, when and where they are going to obtain satisfaction. The most obvious change for retailers in this area has been the increasing demand for convenience. Convenience in terms of time and location has become increasingly important, giving rise to 24-hour trading, petrol station convenience stores, home and workplace delivery, and supermarket retailers at railway stations amongst a range of reactions.

Thirdly, there are changes in *shopping behaviour*, ie the consumer process during the shopping activity itself. As consumers have changed, so the elements of the retail offer that attract them and encourage them to purchase or consume have changed. Much more attention has had to be paid by retailers to elements of store design, ambience and smell, as well as issues to do with the balance between price, service and quality. For many, going shopping has sometimes become more of a leisure activity.

Combining these various strands of consumer change, we can suggest that there are now different reasons behind different food shopping trips and that consumers satisfy their desires in different ways and at different times (see Table 2.2). At some times, consumers need to replenish basic items and the trip is a highly functional one. At other times similar items may be purchased using a different method, eg the same consumer might buy the same goods from a Tesco superstore, a Tesco Metro or Tesco.com, but at different times. Other shopping trips are focused on the trip itself more than the shopping. Leisure in its broadest sense is critical to the experience of the trip and of the shopping. Consumers and their changing behaviours are much more complex than they have been in the past, and meeting consumers' demands is harder.

The changes outlined above are derived particularly from a consideration of Europe. They are, however, also instantly recognizable to other developed economies such as the USA and Japan (see Larke and Causton, 2005; Seth and Randall, 2005). With the increasingly global nature of the large-scale retail battleground, however, such trends are also found in economies across the developing world (Dawson and Lee, 2004; Dawson *et al*, 2003), including Brazil, China, Taiwan, South Korea and South Africa, and are beginning to be felt in countries such

Table 2.2   Types of food shopping trips

Purpose	Reason	Product Example	Retailer and Format Example
Essential	Replenishment of stock items; primary food shopping trip.	Food and household items.	Food superstore or supermarket.
Purposive	Clear purpose to trip; big items.	Food and household items; Christmas purchases.	Food superstore.
Leisure (or fun)	Social activity, occasionally ancillary to visit.	Specialized food products; factory or farm visits.	Farm shops; farmers' market; delicatessen.
Convenience	Time constrained; top-up trip; everyday purchases.	Ready meals; milk; newspapers.	Convenience store; petrol station store; city centre store; local shop
Experimental	Unusual product or innovative method.	Home delivery of standard order; local produce; specialized food products.	Specialized farm shop; Tesco.com; Organics Direct; Whole Foods.

as India and Russia, as well as Dubai and Saudi Arabia. Wherever we look, (fresh) food retailing is being altered by global and local developmental dynamics. Less obviously, perhaps, the supply systems needed to meet these demands are also undergoing transformation.

These changes in culture and consumers have important implications for retailers in terms of what is actually sold in fresh food. The developments have placed an emphasis on the availability of products and the need for an effective supply chain. At the same time, the range of products to be carried and the varying sizes of packaging and quantities for sale add complication to the logistics task.

RETAIL LOCATIONS AND OUTLETS

This emphasis on culture and consumers is reflected in the importance that is afforded by retailers to the places where retailing takes place – the location of retailing. This is in itself a distinctive dimension of the retail industry, as few industries involve such a diverse and dispersed type of outlet network. There are, for example, almost 30,000 Seven-Eleven convenience stores across the world, with over 11,000 in Japan alone. Ahold at one time had over 9,000 stores in 28 countries on four continents. It is hard to conceive of other businesses outside retailing having such extensive branch networks to control. Whilst the old adage 'location, location, location' has probably been overplayed, it has some truth, and above all it is an identifying characteristic of the retail trade. Retailers must understand the spaces within which consumers operate and try to match these in terms of their locational and operational decisions. Retailers thus manage the macro-location (the country, region or city) and the micro-location (the store location and internal environment).

Retailing not only has a distinctive locational dimension, but also is further distinguished by its diversity of retail location. Furthermore, locations are dynamic. Some shop locations seem fixed in the most visible of ways, as with Harrods in London, Galeries Lafayette and Printemps in Paris or Bloomingdales in New York. Others are more transient, such as wet or night markets, car-boot sales, farmers' markets and other similar activities. Whilst some street locations clearly have a premium for retail activity, such as Ginza in Tokyo, Oxford Street in London or 5th Avenue in New York, others come and go from retail activity. Town centres and city centres are for many economies the main place of concentration of retailing and the centre of this economic and social interaction. Market spaces in historic cities such as Istanbul illustrate this well. Neighbourhood stores or corner shops have a similar function on a different scale. In most Western economies, this central emphasis has been disturbed by the decentralization of much retail (and particularly food retail) activity (Longstreth, 1997, 1999), and similar processes are now under way across the globe. The largest shopping centres being constructed are all, for example, in the Asian market.

This movement away from central locations has been encouraged by a number of factors, including:

- the growth of an affluent and mobile population in suburban areas in contrast to a declining less affluent and less mobile town and city centre population;

- the development of strong corporate chains with fewer ties to a locality and more willingness and need to move shops to areas of demand and opportunity;

- changes in the methods of selling, which have seen a demand for larger stores and associated parking. Such stores are harder to accommodate in built-up areas and have been cheaper to build and operate in decentralized locations.

This decentralization has been controversial, as it utilizes greenfield land in many instances, often has an adverse aesthetic impact and expands the reliance on private transport. Operationally it can have many benefits. Consumers have certainly embraced it. As a consequence, some locations, in both urban and rural situations, have seen a huge reduction in retail outlets and consequent problems of accessibility and choice for consumers who are not mobile (economically or physically). Land-use planners have therefore been increasingly concerned to integrate retail development within existing towns and cities (Davies, 1995; Guy, 1994). Nonetheless, across much of Europe the policies of the 1980s and 1990s have resulted in large numbers of decentralized food and non-food superstores. In developing countries such as Thailand and Malaysia there is much concern about the impact on local small-scale retailers of new (Western) out-of-town and large stores. Because of this there is a debate about the need to prohibit or at least slow down such developments, despite the benefits seen by consumers and the economy.

The food superstore or hypermarket has become the dominant retail format across many developed (and increasingly developing) countries. The combination of a very large store, often single-storey in design, with lots of associated car parking, in locations away from traditional centres, has become common and highly successful (Sparks, 2000b). It has to a considerable degree transformed our perception of food and grocery retailing. Whilst such stores are increasingly resisted due to perceived impacts on the environment and on existing trading formats and centres, their sheer number means they have huge importance. They have also set standards for presentation, range and supply that other formats and forms have had to follow. This has allowed a better understanding of the scope for compromise in the basic model of the hypermarket or large supermarket. New stores may often be found on two levels, with public transport interchanges, and increasingly have more associated non-food developments. To compete with such stores, existing retailers and smaller formats have had to improve their efficiency and effectiveness, though in many countries they combine this with a desire for legal protection from competition by the government.

The development of the food superstore concentrated the location of consumer spending. The demands are thus very high for products and availability is a key. The superstore though is not simply a volume replacement for a number of smaller stores. Many of these superstores are purpose built and have developed efficient unloading systems and separated consumer and distribution interactions. The straightforward modernization of delivery to superstores encouraged reconsideration of other channel activities (Smith and Sparks, 1993).

SHOPKEEPERS AND RETAIL MANAGERS

The nature of retail business is also distinctive and diverse in terms of those who take on the management and operation of retail businesses – the shopkeepers and retail managers. The organizational or firm type has implications for resources, the scope of operation and decision-making roles and capabilities. Retailing remains numerically dominated in almost every country by independent retailers, ie retailers who operate single stores with shopkeepers who are the owners and/or managers. This local form of retailing has been central to retail operations throughout history. Retailing has low entry and exit barriers. However, the independent retailer is but one form of business organization in retailing. Five forms are generally identified:

- independent traders, eg the local village shop;

- government retail shops, eg Systembolaget AB, and LCBO;

- corporate or multiple retailers, eg ICA Ahold, Tesco, Wal-Mart;

- cooperative chains, eg Coop Norden, the Co-operative Group;

- contractual or franchise chains, eg Spar.

The balance of power amongst these business organizational forms varies from country to country and has altered over time (eg Colla, 2004; Lindblom and Rimstedt, 2004). As a general rule, centrally controlled large organizations (running chains of large and small stores) have gained power and market share from other forms and particularly from independent and cooperative retailers. Corporate retailers have become the dominant commercial form in many countries. This power has been gained because of the cost and efficiency advantages of operating larger businesses under central control. The role and function of store management in a chain organization has consequently become more critical over time, though the boundaries of central versus local control remain flexible and variable amongst companies (Burt and Sparks, 2003).

It should be clear from the discussion thus far that retailing, including food retailing, has been transformed in many ways. This transformation necessarily extends to the management of retail businesses. As the scale of the retail store has increased and as the scale of the retail business has grown, so too the need for professional, well-trained management has expanded. The types of skills and demands that a store manager in any organizational type has to exhibit are now very different to those required of the shopkeepers of old. Local shopkeepers now compete in a massively competitive industry, where professional store management and control principles and techniques have developed strongly.

For example, Wal-Mart is the world's largest retailer and company. It had sales in 2004 (ie the financial year ending 31 January 2005) of $285 billion operated over 5,300 stores, employed over 1.5 million associates, and made over $17 billion operating profit. Wal-Mart reached the landmark of $1 billion annual sales in 1979 and then achieved $1 billion sales in a week in 1993, before taking $1 billion sales *in a day* in 2001.

If it were a country, Wal-Mart would be the 21st largest economy in the world – ranked just behind Taiwan and ahead of Austria. If its rivals wished to eclipse it in sales terms, then an unlikely alliance of Carrefour, Metro, Ahold and Kroger would be required. If all its employees resigned overnight, it could fill its vacancies by hiring Iceland and Estonia.

(*M&M Planet Retail*, October 2004, p 17)

This is the extreme scale of organization against which a local independent shopkeeper competes.

At the store level, a large UK food hypermarket could take well over £100 million in a year in sales. The store could be open 24 hours a day, seven days a week. There might be over 750 employees on the site working a variety of shift patterns and at many different grades. The amount of product and consumers passing in and out of the store in a day is huge. The technology in the store is highly advanced and sophisticated. Its stores, marketing, buying and logistics operations are all professional and dynamic environments. Modern retailing has some of the most exacting, exciting and well-paid jobs in any country and has become increasingly reliant on professional staff, throughout the organization and beyond. In terms of fresh food channels, this professionalism is exhibited by buyers, distributors and shop staff in providing a high-quality product for consumers.

PRODUCT SOURCING AND DISTRIBUTION

The growth of large retail companies such as Wal-Mart, Tesco, Aldi or Carrefour (Seth and Randall, 2005) also illustrates another fundamental difference between retailing and other forms of business. To a much greater extent than, for example, in manufacturing, retailers have to construct structures for managing multi-plant operations with much greater variety and variability in concept and transactions. Retail management at the highest level is very different to other production-based businesses and is at the local level much more open to local demand vicissitudes. The role of technology in data capture and transmission and in chain control has therefore increased substantially.

The business of retailing involves the selection and assembly of goods for sale, ie the process of product sourcing and distribution. This process is also one dominated by variety – of types of goods, sourcing strategy and product mix. Retailers sell a wide variety of items. Some are concentrated in a narrow line of business (specialist stores, eg Oddbins), whereas others are much wider in their scope (general stores, eg Asda/Wal-Mart Supercenter). The balance amongst items may change for some retailers over time. In any event, retailers have to obtain sources for their product range. This involves the retailers themselves dealing with particular suppliers (perhaps local suppliers), with a wholesaler or some other form of intermediary.

The products that are sourced have changed over time. Whilst there always has been a market for exotic and non-local product, the expectations of many consumers and the abilities of many retailers have transformed the supply position. A reliance on local (ie immediate area) sourcing is now not the normal relationship. For many retailers, products from around the world are standard elements to be included in the product mix. This is as much the case in fresh food as it is in non-food products. This has impacts on the situation of agriculture and supply systems in host countries (Dolan and Humphrey, 2000; Hughes, 2000; Weatherspoon and Reardon, 2003).

As retailers have become larger and as their abilities have increased, they have been better able to exploit international product sourcing and buying opportunities. For many products, the costs of production are much lower in countries outside the developed world and it therefore makes economic sense to manufacture abroad and transport the product. Any British supermarket contains many non-UK or non-EU products. Control of the supply chain is thus vital to get products to the stores in good condition. This process of retailer control of supply systems and the use of computer technology for control of central distribution have been key features of recent years. British food retailers' logistics systems are amongst the most efficient in the world as a consequence (Fernie and Sparks, 2004; Fernie and Staines, 2001; McKinsey, 1998).

In obtaining products, retailers have a choice to make over what products to sell, but also under what name to sell them. This might be simply the choice of the name of the store, but retailers have also themselves become names or brands of note. The approach to retailer branding varies across the globe, but large retailers are becoming much more concerned in managing their own retail names or brand (Burt and Sparks, 2002). In the United Kingdom, retailers such as Tesco have developed a very extensive and sophisticated branding strategy, which has allowed them to leverage their name and reputation into sectors other than their core business. In food retailing in the UK, retailer brands (what others term own-label or private label) have become dominant. Product supply is thus even more within the retailers' control, and advertising and promotion are constantly reinforcing the corporate brand. The retailer has become the brand and is trusted by the consumer. This has allowed brand extension into services and brand disaggregation in the core food business (see Table 2.3). Most UK food retailers now have a structured branding approach targeting specific consumer segments. Consistency, reliability and quality of supply are thus critical.

Table 2.3 UK grocery retail branding price segmentation in 2004

	Exclusive	*Standard*	*Value*
Tesco	Finest	Tesco	Value
Sainsbury	Taste the Difference	Sainsbury's	Economy
Asda	Extra Special	Asda	Smart Price

Note: This table is constructed on the basis of product price points. It excludes alternative branding concepts based on other product attributes such as health (eg Sainsbury's Be Good to Yourself and Tesco Healthy Eating), organic origin (eg all company retailer organic brands) or other segments (eg Sainsbury's Blue Parrot Café brand of healthy eating products for children).

BUSINESS RELATIONSHIPS

The process of retailing involves relationships with other businesses and groups. These too have their own distinctive characteristics arising from the nature of retailing. The requirement to source products, combined with issues over branding, inevitably means that retailers are concerned with relationships with business partners, as well as relationships with staff and consumers. These business relationships can take many forms and many variants, but essentially retailers can choose to have administered, collaborative or transactional (sometimes conflictual) relationships (Dawson and Shaw, 1990; Duffy and Fearne, 2004). In short, retailers can either work with partners to achieve shared objectives or they can use their position alone simply to operate the business to achieve their own ends.

For example, product sourcing involves a number of elements, but retailers are attempting to purchase and obtain product at a given price and quality position. For some retailers, price is the overriding concern and retailers will always seek the lowest price for products they know their customers will purchase. This means that the relationships they have with individual suppliers may be transient and focus on transactional price components alone. The relationship in that sense is straightforward, but often comes down to a conflict about price.

More complex, but of importance to many retailers, is the notion of a collaborative relationship with suppliers, which involves all parties in something rather more than simply a transaction based on price. The relationship might be to secure a source of supply or to obtain a given quality and quantity of a product. It might be to develop a product line or to ensure product consistency and quality, or to allow access to a unique product. If a retailer is branding the product then the collaborative arrangement may be about ensuring certain standards. For many retailers, therefore, whilst price may well be very important, there could well be other aspects of the business relationship that need to be in place. Some of these relationships or partnerships are of long standing and have involved extensive product development and consequent growth of both partners. Thus, in food retailing, some retail brand manufacturing companies such as Northern Foods have become highly significant and large businesses in their own right, primarily through this collaborative arrangement for retailer brand production over a long time period. Inevitably such a relationship asks questions of existing practices in supply chains, particularly when the point of production could be anywhere in the world.

Retailers, of course, have business relationships beyond product sourcing. Relationships exist with an array of service providers depending on the operation. Finance is one example of such relationships, with independent retailers seeking bank finance and multiple or corporate retailers searching for institutional finance to enable them to develop their store portfolios. With retail sites being highly expensive to rent, buy or develop, retailers need to secure such institutional funding.

One of the most important relationships occurs in the physical supply of products to the retailer. Product sourcing in a transactional sense has been identified above, but products have to be delivered to the retail store to be available for merchandising and for sale. Logistics systems and logistics providers therefore may be key components of another set of business relationships. Whilst we may see many vehicles on the roads carrying retailer logos and livery, many of them are owned and operated by contractual logistics services partners such as Exel in the UK.

As might be imagined, with product sourcing complexities, expansion in the number of stores and spatial breadth in many companies, and the increased expectations of consumers with respect to product quality and availability, logistics supply systems have become more and more important. For many retailers, being in retailing is sufficient, and logistics systems are often outsourced to these logistics services providers. In many cases, their specialist handling skills are essential to the supply systems. Outsourcing, however, is not a question of 'out of sight, out of mind' but rather is a managed partnership to ensure appropriately effective and efficient supply of products.

MERCHANDISING AND SELLING

For many outside retailing, selling is often viewed as the same as retailing, but selling is but one component of the retail operation. Selling itself varies of course, with the move to self-service in many product categories and retailers reducing the sales role in the store. In other retailers, the skills of the sales staff are critical in the delivery of customer service and the repeat patronage of consumers. The art and science of selling and the quality of the sales staff are of fundamental importance for much business success. In other situations, the lack of quality or knowledge of the staff acts as a negative influence on consumers.

Store and selling design varies enormously by situation (Underhill, 1999). The emphasis on design, staff knowledge and staff competency may be vital in some situations, but of no consequence in others. The retail offer has become more disparate overall as retailers have attempted to match their offer to the demands of the customer. Some stores are dramatic (eg Whole Foods) whilst others are highly functional (eg Aldi or Lidl). Some have many staff selling; others simply have takers of money. All, however, are based on retailers' understanding of what works with their customers.

Store-based selling has its own distinctive characteristics. How the product is merchandised and the ways in which design and display interact are important to attracting consumers and obtaining their custom. As a result, much effort is expended in laying out the store and in ensuring that products are presented appropriately. This presentation includes aspects of visual display, as well as essential product information. Depending on the product lines involved and the approach of the retailer, such merchandising may be of lesser or greater importance. Even in supposedly simple retailer situations, eg markets, product display can be sophisticated and help consumers make choices amongst 'stores' and products. The differences in approach to merchandising can be seen in Figures 2.1 to 2.4. These figures also show how

Figure 2.1   *Whole Foods fresh foods presentation* (source: *author photograph, 2002*)

Figure 2.2   *Fresh food presentation in Albert Heijn, The Netherlands*
(source: *author photograph, 2005*)

Figure 2.3   *Fresh food presentation in Tesco* (source: *author photograph, 2001*)

Figure 2.4   *Fresh food presentation in Giant, Singapore* (source: *author photograph, 2002*)

supply system techniques and packaging can flow through to the shop floor, and are part of the merchandising presentation in some stores, for good or bad, dependent on the consumer target market.

Store merchandising and display techniques condition the retail environment in every store. Some of the techniques are rather obvious and relatively easy to identify, whereas others are far more subtle and difficult to discern (Underhill, 1999). Visual merchandising and design direct your attention and your direction of movement by leading you around and through the merchandise. 'Hot spots' in the store are created to drag you through the shop and grab your attention. Lighting and music are used in some stores to alter the mood of parts of shops. Colour is used to create an environment or an image. Touch is encouraged to exploit the tactile senses. Even smells are use to evoke responses, whether it be perfume, cosmetics or coffee and fresh bread. Some design and display is organized to recreate remembered activities or past situations. In short, stores are not abstract collections of products, but managed selling environments, designed to stimulate customer reactions and purchase.

Fresh food is therefore sold in a managed selling environment, and the visual presentation of the product is of importance to the retailer and the consumer. There is a requirement for the presentation of the product to be assisted or, at least, not hindered by the packaging and handling systems. Fresh food needs to look 'right', and thus quality of product and of presentation is of considerable importance. Handling systems can help this process if carefully designed.

CHANGE IN FOOD RETAILING: SUMMARY

The description so far of the process of change in food retailing has pointed both to the major functional areas of retail business activity and to some of the changes that have been taking place in the sector. Any analysis of major recent trends in retailing (see the box below) produces quite an extensive list of transformations and issues.

Major retail trends of the 1990s/2000s

- A decrease in the total number of shops.

- An increase in the number of large food and non-food superstores.

- New shopping centres.

- Growth of retail sales and floorspace.

- Low levels of inflation.

- Increase in small store formats.

- Concentration in retail sales.

- Extensions of product ranges in superstores.

- Strengthening of primary locations and weakening of tertiary ones.

- Large retailers taking control of the supply chain.

- Changes in accessibility to retail provision.

- Increased use of sophisticated technologies by retailers.

- More variety of potential locations.

- Wider use of town centre management.

- More awareness of retailer activity.

Source: After Dawson (2000)

The listing in the box is readily recognizable in developed economies, but similar trends are now being found in many economies (Dawson and Burt, 1998; Dawson *et al*, 2003; Larke and Causton, 2005; Seth and Randall, 2005). We can, however, condense this listing into three key areas.

First, it is clear that we have in recent decades lived through an enormous change in the *location* of retailing. Food retailing takes place now in very different locations from previously. We have already discussed the broad trends of decentralization of retail location and the rise of superstores. Retailing has been locationally transformed. From a channel perspective this may have had advantages for the distribution of fresh food products.

Secondly, there has been an alteration in the *format* through which food retailing takes place. Shops today are not like shops of previous times, and retailer strategies have become more segmented. They differ in scale, design, technique and approach. This is obvious in terms of the larger store formats, but is equally true for smaller formats. A common component, however, is the improvement in the quality of provision.

Thirdly, it has been emphasized that food retailers *have increased in scale and power* (Burt and Sparks, 2003; Seth and Randall, 1999, 2005). They have grown enormously in size and now are major businesses in their own right, often being larger than the manufacturers who supply them. They can thus reorganize various relationships to suit themselves. This scale of operation brings practical and financial benefits to the business. Recently, we have seen the scale increase another level with major mergers or takeovers on the international stage, eg Wal-Mart of Woolco in Canada, Asda in the UK and Seiyu in Japan; the merger of Carrefour and Promodès in France; and the expansion of Ahold and Delhaize across the world (though scale alone may not always guarantee success). The world's leading retailers are now amongst some of the biggest organizations around and have an increasingly international approach. Their professionalized management approach has changed the sector and its supply systems.

One of the key themes that implicitly underlies this chapter is that, if there has been a transformation at the retail shop end of the channel, then there has to be a transformation in supply systems as well (Sparks, 1998). To meet consumers' demands for new products in new formats and in new ways, the supply system has had to be reorganized and refocused. This reorganization is needed because the nature of retailing and supply has changed. Retailers through their knowledge of consumers have gained power and used this power in a variety of ways. One of these methods has been through the reorganization of fresh food channels and the adoption of supply chain management principles to gain efficiency and effectiveness. It is to this that we now turn.

3 Fresh Food Retail Logistics

All of us perhaps take for granted that products will be available to buy in the shops. The cornucopia of products that are available in a supermarket sometimes masks the hard work that goes into getting the right products to the right place at the right time and in the right condition. We expect to find a wide range of good-quality food and groceries, and that our food will both be fresh and have a suitable shelf-life. With the introduction of e-commerce, we have come to expect 24-hour delivery of products from across the world, and home delivery of groceries from the local Tesco at a time of our choosing.

As we have suggested in Chapter 2, consumers' willingness to wait to be satisfied or served is reduced and they expect and demand instant product availability and gratification. If all this has changed, then it should be obvious that the supply or logistics system that gets products from production through retailing to consumption has also had to be reconfigured. This transformation (Fernie and Sparks, 2004; Sparks, 1998) derives from cost and service requirements in addition to consumer and retailer change. Elements of logistics are remarkably expensive, if not controlled effectively. Holding stock or inventory in warehouses just in case it is needed is a highly costly activity. The stock itself is expensive and might not sell or could become obsolete or, in the case of food, 'go off'. Warehouses generally are expensive to build and maintain as well as operate. Vehicles to transport goods between warehouses and stores are major costs, in terms of both capital and running costs, with drivers' wages and ever higher fuel prices. The packaging and handling systems in supply systems can themselves be costly and/or add costs to the movement and storage of products. There is thus an imperative to making sure that logistics is carried out effectively and efficiently.

At the same time, if logistics is made more effective and efficient, then as well as cost reductions there can be service benefits. By appropriate integration of demand and supply, mainly through the widespread use of information technology and appropriate handling systems, retailers can provide a better service to consumers by, for example, having fresher, higher-quality produce arriving to meet consumer demand. With the appropriate logistics, products should be of a better presentational quality and could possibly be cheaper and have a longer shelf-life, and there should be far fewer instances of stockouts, ie product unavailability or gaps on the store shelves. If operating properly, a good logistics system can both reduce costs and improve service, providing a competitive advantage for the retailer.

The role of logistics and the way in which logistics is changing in fresh food retailing are the central components of this chapter. Building on the discussion of the growth and use of retail scale and power and the rise of new retail formats and locations, this chapter examines first the components of the logistics task and the nature of the retail-led logistics transformation. This is followed by more detailed examination of a key element of fresh food supply, namely the requirements of temperature controlled supply chains.

THE LOGISTICS TASK

Retailing and logistics are concerned with product availability. Many have described this as 'getting the right products to the right place at the right time' (eg Fisher, Raman and McClelland, 2000). Unfortunately, however, that description does not do justice to the amount of effort that has to go into a logistics supply system and the multitude of ways that the supply systems can go wrong. The very simplicity of the statement suggests logistics is an easy process. The real trick, however, is making logistics look easy, day in and day out, whilst reacting to a volatile and changing consumer demand. For example, if the temperature rises and the sun comes out in an untypical Scottish summer, then demand for ice cream, soft drinks and even salad items rises dramatically. How do retailers make sure they remain in stock to capture this fluctuating demand?

The example above demonstrates that retailers must be concerned with the flows of product *and* information within the business and the supply chain. In order to make products available, retailers have to manage their logistics in terms of product movement and demand management. They need to know what is selling in the stores and both anticipate and react quickly to changes in this demand. At the same time they need to be able to move less demand-volatile products in an efficient and cost-effective manner.

The logistics management task is therefore concerned with managing the components of the 'logistics mix'. Table 3.1 identifies five components. It should be clear that all of these elements are inter-linked. If a retailer gets good data on demand from its checkout system, then the scheduling of transport and the level of stock holding become more straightforward. If the level of inventory can be reduced, then perhaps fewer warehouses are needed. If communications and transport can be highly effectively linked, then perhaps a retailer can move from putting stock away in a warehouse to running a distribution centre that sorts products for immediate store delivery, ie approaching a 'just-in-time' system.

It should also be clear that retailers may not do all of this on their own. Retailers are involved in the selling of goods and services to the consumer. For this they take product from manufacturers and suppliers. Retailers thus have a direct interest in the logistics systems of their suppliers. If a retailer is effective, but its suppliers are not, then errors and delays in supply from the manufacturer will impact the retailer and the retailer's consumers, in terms of either higher prices or stockouts (no products available on the store shelves). If a retailer can integrate its logistics system with that of its suppliers, then such problems can be minimized. Much more importantly, however, the entire supply chain can then be optimized and managed as a single entity. This brings potential advantages of costs reduction *and* service enhancement, not only for the retailer, but also for the supplier. It should also mean that products reach the stores more rapidly, thus better meeting fluctuating customer demand.

For example, Tesco, by working with producers of fresh foods, eg lettuce, can ensure that products are picked in reaction to demand levels and distributed through the distribution centres rapidly, ie not

Table 3.1   Components of the 'logistics mix'

Component	Description
Storage Facilities	These might be warehouses or distribution centres or simply the stock rooms of retail stores. Retailers manage these facilities to enable them to keep stock in anticipation of, or to react to, demand for products. Increasingly, some centres are run 'stock-less' and act as sortation hubs.
Inventory	All retailers hold stock to some extent. The question for retailers is the amount of stock or inventory (finished products and/or component parts) that has to be held for each product and the location of this stock to meet demand changes.
Transportation	Most products have to be transported in some way at some stage of their journey from production to consumption. Retailers therefore have to manage a transport operation that might involve different forms of transport, different sizes of vehicles and different scheduling availability of drivers, vehicles and even store access.
Unitization and Packaging	Consumers generally buy products in small quantities. They sometimes make purchase decisions based on product looks and packaging. Retailers are deeply concerned to get products that are easy to handle in logistics terms, don't cost too much to package or handle, yet retain their selling ability on shelves. Secondary and transit packaging can be a cost to the supply chain and is increasingly replaced by returnable handling systems where possible. Unitization is combined with standardization to provide order to the handling of products.
Communications	To get products to where we want them, it is necessary to have information, about both demand and supply, but also about volumes, stock, prices and movements. Retailers have thus become increasingly concerned with being able to capture data at appropriate points in the supply and demand system and, most importantly, to use that information to have a more efficient and effective logistics operation.

stored. If the foods are in the shop more quickly, the freshness is maximized and shelf-life is extended. The consumer gets a better-quality product but at the same time wastage costs are reduced. The system is cheaper but also provides a better service.

This description of the logistics task is immediately recognizable. However, it does tend to gloss over the importance of unitization and packaging. Products appear to move seamlessly from production to the retail store and shop floor. This is, of course, far from the truth. In reality, products have to be organized and handled in order to make this journey. If organized efficiently then there are costs and service benefits. If there is a lack of supply chain agreement on appropriate sizing and handling then time and cost will be lost. This search for efficiency and effectiveness through packaging and standardization in handling is at the heart of packaging logistics.

Products when produced have to be packaged and/or handled in some way. Decisions about the size and shape of packaging and the information it carries are important to handling throughout the supply chain. How many products make up various packaging sizes is a fundamental question. Similarly, if standard handling systems can be adopted then systems can be built around the sizes and processes. In environmental terms returnable or reusable handling systems may reduce the amount of transport packaging and be more environmentally sustainable. These issues form the basis of the next chapter and to a considerable extent the remainder of the book.

Summarizing, the logistics task can be described (Christopher, 1998: 4) as: 'The process of strategically managing the procurement, movement and storage of materials, parts and finished inventory (and the related information flows) through the organisation and its marketing channels in such a way that current and future profitability are maximised through the cost effective fulfilment of orders.'

As retailers have begun to embrace this logistics approach and examine their supply chains, many have realized that, to carry out logistics properly, there has to be a transformation of approach and operations. It is to this we now turn.

RETAIL LOGISTICS TRANSFORMATION

When Tesco opened their new 16,000 square foot store in Leicester in 1961, they claimed it was the largest grocery store in Europe. Today, Tesco's *average* store size in the UK is almost twice this and, in Eastern

Europe, Tesco are opening hypermarkets 10 times as large as this pioneering store. It should be obvious that the scale, location and product range of the 1961 Leicester store and their newest Polish hypermarket reflect major shifts in the retail form. The average Wal-Mart Supercenter is approaching 200,000 square feet in size. It should be clear that the supply systems for such stores also represent a fundamental shift in operations and approach. New store formats demand new logistics. The logistics required for a new hypermarket is vastly different to the logistics required for the stores it replaces. Such differences are one component of the logistics transformation. It is as essential, as well, that existing stores and new smaller formats also have effective supply systems to meet their new requirements and demands.

Such new stores, which we see across Europe and increasingly elsewhere in the world, also represent visible reminders of the change in power. Retailers have grown substantially in scale as businesses. This growth has been greater than the growth that has taken place in manufacturers. This scale imbalance has been combined with the better understanding of consumers that retailers can gain through closeness to customers and through technology. Manufacturers are a step removed from this customer demand. With better data and greater scale, combined in the UK in some sectors with a massive development of retailer branding, retailers have been able to wrest and then maintain control over distribution channels and logistics activities, though the relationships are uneven (Burt and Sparks, 2003; Ogbonna and Wilkinson, 1996).

Retailers were once effectively the passive recipients of manufacturers' products, allocated to stores by the manufacturers in anticipation of demand. Today, retailers are the active controllers of product supply in reaction to known customer demand. They control, organize and manage the supply chain from production to consumption. This is the essence of the retail logistics transformation that has taken place. Retailers are the channel captains and set the pace in logistics. Having extended their channel control and focused on efficiency and effectiveness, retailers are now attempting to engender a more cooperative and collaborative stance in many aspects of logistics. They are recognizing that there are still gains to be made on standards and efficiency, but that these are probably only obtained as channel gains (ie in association with manufacturers and logistics services providers) rather than at the single-firm level.

Table 3.2 charts this history of innovation in logistics by major grocery retailers. The stages are characterized by a movement from a

Table 3.2   Major logistics innovations by multiple grocery retailers

Period	Problem	Innovation	Consequences
1960s and 1970s	Disorderly delivery by suppliers to supermarkets; queues of vehicles led to both inefficiency and disruption.	Introduction of regional distribution centres (RDCs) to channel goods from suppliers to supermarkets operated by retailers.	1) Strict timing of supplier delivery to RDC imposed by retailers. 2) Retailers build and operate RDC. 3) Retailer operates own delivery fleet between RDC and supermarkets within its catchment area.
1980s	Retailers becoming too committed to operating logistics services in support of retail activity.	Operations of retailer-owned RDCs and vehicle fleets outsourced to specialist freight companies.	1) Retailers can concentrate on 'core business' of retailing. 2) Retailer achieves better financial return from capital investment in supermarkets than in RDCs and vehicles.
1980s and 1990s	Available floorspace at retail outlets being underused; too much floorspace used for storage.	Conversion of storage floorspace at supermarkets to sales floorspace; corporate strategy and brand development; reusable transit packaging.	1) Better sales revenue potential at retail outlets. 2) RDCs absorb products formerly kept in-store at supermarkets. 3) Just-in-time (JIT) delivery used from RDC to replenish supermarket shelves.
1990s and 2000s	Requirement for better customer service and cost control over a range of retail formats and channels; range of products expands.	Reorganization of RDCs; some development of stock-less centres; store-based internet delivery systems; development of Efficient Consumer Response (ECR); concentration on flow-through processes and store-specific distribution; factory gate pricing; retail ready and 'one-touch' packaging.	1) Better in-store quality and stock position. 2) Technological expansion through operations. 3) Rapid roll-out of internet operations. 4) More efficient replenishment and less store effort.

Source: After Cooper, Browne and Peters (1991)

manufacturer-controlled, transport-oriented system to a retail-led and replenishment-focused technology-rich supply chain. This transformation began in the food retail sector. Figure 3.1 shows the effect this assertion of leadership and maintenance of control has had on the stock-holding levels of Tesco (see also Smith, 1998; Smith and Sparks, 1993, 2004). The figure visibly illustrates the shift from disorderly systems through the enhancement-of-efficiency phase to the current low-stock position (with recent increases accounted for by the developments in non-food and global retailing expansion).

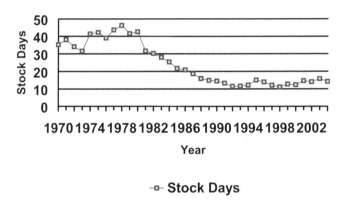

Figure 3.1   *Stock days in Tesco 1970–2005*

McKinnon (1996) reviewed and summarized the key components of this logistics transformation, primarily in the context of the United Kingdom. He identified six trends, all of which are closely related and mutually reinforcing (see also Table 3.2):

1. Retailers increased their control over secondary distribution (ie warehouse to shop) by channelling an increasing proportion of their supplies through distribution centres (DCs). In the grocery sector this process is now virtually complete. British retailers exert much tighter control over the supply chain than their counterparts in most other countries. Their logistical operations are heavily dependent on information technology (IT), particularly the large integrated stock replenishment systems that control the movement and storage of an enormous number of separate products.

2. Restructured retailers' logistical systems have reduced inventory and generally improved efficiency through the development of

'composite distribution' (the distribution of mixed-temperature items through the same distribution centre and on the same vehicle) and centralization in specialist warehouses of slower-moving stock. In the case of mixed retail businesses, the establishment of 'common stock rooms' (where stock is shared across a number of stores, with demand deciding to which store stock is allocated) is developed.

3. There has been an adoption of 'quick response' (QR) type approaches with the aim of cutting inventory levels and improving speed of product flow. This has involved reducing order lead time and moving to a more frequent delivery of smaller consignments both internally (between DC and shop) and on external links with suppliers. This has greatly increased the rate of stock turn and increased the production of supplies being 'cross-docked', rather than stored, at DCs. QR was made possible by the development of electronic data interchange (EDI) and electronic point of sale (EPOS), the latter driving the 'sales-based ordering' (SBO) systems that most of the larger retailers have installed. In other words, as an item is sold and scanned in a shop, these data are used to inform replenishment and reordering systems and thus to react quickly to demand. Sharing such data with key suppliers further integrates production with the supply function. Major British retailers have been faster to adopt these technologies than many counterparts in other European countries, though the technologies still have to diffuse to many medium-sized and small retail businesses.

4. There has been rationalization of primary distribution (ie factory to warehouse). Partly as a result of QR pressures and partly as a result of intensifying competition, retailers have extended their control upstream of the DC (ie from the DC to the manufacturer). In an effort to improve the utilization of their logistical assets, many have integrated their secondary and primary distribution operations and run them as a single 'network system'. This reduces waste and improves efficiency. This rationalization of primary distribution has now been taken a stage further within the UK as retailers implement factory gate pricing (primary distribution) with their suppliers. This strategy (ex-works costing) extends the retailers' control over the flow and transportation of goods from the supplier. The retailer decides which companies should be doing the transport and also the shape of the consolidation of suppliers and their products.

5. Supply chain management (SCM) and efficient consumer response (ECR) have been introduced. Having improved the efficiency of their logistics operations, many retailers have closely collaborated with suppliers to maximize the efficiency of the retail supply chain as a whole. SCM and ECR provide a management framework within which retailer and suppliers can more effectively coordinate their activities. The underpinning technologies for ECR have been well established in the United Kingdom, so conditions have been ripe for the application of this principle.

6. There is an increased return flow of packaged material and handling equipment for recycling/reuse. Retailers have become much more heavily involved in this 'reverse logistics' operation. This trend has been reinforced by the introduction of the EU Packaging Directive. Although the United Kingdom has lagged behind other European countries, particularly Germany, in this field, there remain opportunities to develop reusable containers and reverse logistics systems to manage their circulation.

Whilst McKinnon's analysis was developed in the context of the United Kingdom, such trends are being found in many other countries. This diffusion of logistics approaches has occurred for two main reasons. First, the benefits from reconfiguring the supply chain are recognizable from the results achieved. As with much in retailing, therefore, there has been a spate of 'copying' or replication. Secondly, the process of retail internationalization has itself gone beyond simply opening shops in another country. As retailers have internationalized, so they have used their power and position to redevelop and export supply chain practices. Thus, the Tesco systems in Poland and Thailand are based on practices in the United Kingdom. For Wal-Mart, the ability to export its 'model' of business, including its supply chain, is fundamental to its chances of success in international markets.

It should be clear from the discussion above that the modern retail logistics system is heavily dependent on the use of information technology. Logistics now is as much about information movement as it is about product movement. Of course, it remains true that products have to be distributed. Vehicles, packages, boxes and crates are still involved. But, increasingly, data and its use drive logistics and organize what gets moved, when it moves and the form in which it is moved and stored.

The discussion above indicates that modern retail logistics is no longer a separate or functionally based activity. Within a company, warehousing and transport cannot exist as private separate operations. Instead logistics is all about integration, not only within a company, but also increasingly outside the business with suppliers, logistics services providers and customers. Partnership is a strong component of modern retail logistics, and an ability to work with other individuals and other companies is fundamental to success. This of necessity will involve discussions about packaging and handling systems.

It should also have become apparent that the 'reach' of retail logistics has expanded enormously. Companies used to have to manage local supplies and product from local warehouses. Nowadays, retailers are much more international and global in their outlook. Product is sourced from around the world, and so the interactions and movements involved in logistics are now equally international and global. Yet, at the same time, there is concern to enable local suppliers to participate in such systems and thus to add a point of differentiation.

However, it must not be forgotten that logistics is eventually about the movement of product. Much work is undertaken on improving the mechanics and details of product movement and handling, including packaging. For example, a modern supermarket contains good examples of packaging and handling standardization, the best of which makes handling easier and allows customers to buy direct from the product 'retail-ready' packaging. Vehicle fleets may be equipped with global positioning satellite (GPS) systems and advanced tachograph and communications equipment, allowing real-time driver and vehicle performance monitoring and linking vehicles to stores and other distribution points. The timing of deliveries into 'windows' is critical for product flow and labour scheduling. In distribution centres, voice-activated or -controlled picking has added a degree of accuracy and speed to the process. Shelf-ready merchandising or other 'flow'-based handling systems have also speeded up the processes involved (see Figure 3.2). Such detailed developments remain key elements of supply chain integration.

These concerns and conclusions about retail supply chains are highly relevant to the distribution of fresh food. The changes in supply systems have been extensive, and key detailed decisions about practices, eg in packaging and handling, have had to be made industry-wide. In fresh food, these concerns are exacerbated by the complications of temperature controlled supply chains, and it is to these that we now turn.

Figure 3.2   *The use of 'flow' systems* (source: *author photographs*)

Figure 3.2a   *Tesco bananas 2001*

Figure 3.2b
Tesco bananas 2004

TEMPERATURE CONTROLLED SUPPLY CHAINS

A quick examination of any full-range food superstore immediately brings home the importance of fresh and frozen food to the consumer. As noted in Chapter 2, the modern consumer expects the food in the store to be of good quality, to have a decent shelf-life and to be fit for purpose. Similarly, if the retailer can present products attractively and extend their shelf-life then there is more chance of the products being purchased and satisfying consumer needs. Managing the supply chain to maintain quality and 'fitness' therefore has direct cost and service implications. This process of logistics management, however, is not simply a question of moving box A from field B to store C. Many dimensions have to be managed. One of these dimensions is the need for a proper temperature regime. A food superstore contains products supplied and retailed at a number of different temperatures. Failing to maintain an appropriate temperature control can adversely affect the product's appearance or shelf-life, at one end of the spectrum, or could potentially make consumers ill or even kill them at the other end. Temperature controlled supply chains could be said to be a matter of life or death (Kuznesof and Brennan, 2004).

CH Robinson Worldwide/Iowa State University (2001: 1–2) argue that temperature controlled supply chains are more important than 'ordinary' retail supply chains, as they have inherently more complexity and complications:

The [logistics] challenge is more formidable when the materials and products require temperature control. The shelf life is often short for such products, placing even greater importance on the speed and dependability of the transportation and handling systems. Temperature controlled products also require specialized transportation equipment and storage facilities and closer monitoring of product integrity while in the logistics system.

Adding to the logistics complexity is the seasonal demand for many temperature controlled products... arising from natural production conditions and consumer demand... In addition, carriers of temperature controlled products confront unique requirements and incur greater costs than carriers of dry products.

Some of the uniqueness and increased costs derive from this need to ensure temperature control. There is extra cost incurred in the requirements for handling temperature controlled products, and also in the need to monitor temperature regimes in the supply chain.

What is a temperature controlled supply chain?

At its simplest, a temperature controlled supply chain is a food supply chain that requires food products to be maintained in a temperature controlled environment, rather than exposing them to whatever ambient temperatures prevail at the various stages of the supply chain. This basic description hides, however, an essentially complex and potentially complicated and expensive process. The length and complexity of such a supply chain is determined by the natures and sources of the products, the legal and quality assurance requirements on food safety, and the distribution facilities available from production to consumption.

There are several temperature levels for food to suit different types of product groups: for example, we might identify frozen, cold chill, medium chill and exotic chill. Frozen is minus 25 degrees Celsius for ice cream and minus 18 degrees for other foods and food ingredients. Cold chill is 0 degrees to plus 1 degree for fresh meat and poultry, most dairy and meat-based provisions, most vegetables and some fruit. Medium chill is plus 5 degrees for some pastry-based products, butters, fats and cheeses. Exotic chill is plus 10 to plus 15 degrees for potatoes, eggs, exotic fruit and bananas. If a food supply chain is dedicated to a narrow range of products then the temperature will be set at the level for that product set. If a food supply chain is handling a broad range of products then an optimum temperature or a limited number of different temperature settings is used. Failure to maintain appropriate temperature regimes throughout a product's life can shorten the life of that product (it goes 'off') or adversely affect its quality or fitness for consumption.

From the description of the types of temperature needed and knowledge of the supply chains in food retailing, it should be immediately obvious that the management process in temperature controlled supply chains is a complicated one. Chilling and freezing products are in themselves hard, but maintaining this throughout a product's life and in both storage and transit is complicated. How, for example, can a retailer ensure that products are always under the appropriate temperature regime when they travel from a field in New Zealand to a refrigerator in a house in Auchtermuchty, Fife? How do bananas ripen so as to be available for sale? In addition to complexity, however, we can argue that the temperature controlled supply chain is also an increasingly important channel, both in absolute volume terms and due to risk assessments of chain failure.

The importance of temperature controlled supply chains

The temperature controlled supply chain in food is a significant proportion of the retail food market and one that has been increasing steadily (McKinnon and Campbell, 1998). Frozen food in the UK has been increasing in volume by 3–4 per cent on average per annum for the last 40 years. Developments in products such as ready meals and prepared salads have further expanded the market. Per capita consumption of fruit has risen over the last 20 years in the UK. Analysts see the meal solution sector continuing to increase very rapidly (Gorniak, 2002). 'Fast food' chains have captured a huge market share and are reliant on frozen product. The importance of products requiring temperature control, both to the consumer and to retailers, has thus been increasing and seems set to develop further.

Even products that we take for granted require some form of temperature control. Sandwiches, for example, require chilled storage of ingredients. These are then combined to make the finished product, which in turn requires temperature control storage, distribution and display (Smith, Davies and Bent, 2001). Failure to maintain adequate control (for example, placing prawn sandwiches in the sun) generates obvious risks. More subtly, an inability to maintain temperature control will reduce shelf-life for the product, which is in any case often very limited. This increases wastage and complicates the supply dynamics, adding costs.

This growth in temperature controlled products derives both from changes in consumer behaviour and preferences and from the supply systems' abilities to respond to these changes. For example, consumer lifestyles and shopping patterns have altered dramatically, raising demands for convenience products. Production of ready meals has matched a desire for food heating rather than food preparation. The ability to take a frozen meal from the freezer and microwave it to eat immediately is a response to the need to save time and for convenience. Ready-washed and prepared salads fit the same requirement. Rising fruit consumption reflects successive healthy eating campaigns, though in the UK the national diet is low on fruit and vegetables. At the same time, greater concern over freshness of products such as fruit, meat and fish has focused attention on their handling in the supply chain.

On the supply side, changes in the location of product sources and the removal of wholesalers from the channel have had major effects. Technological changes in production and distribution have also allowed a transformation of the supply network. As production and distribution technological capabilities have developed, so the ability for national and international, rather than local, sourcing and distribution has emerged. Products can be brought across the world to satisfy demands for products 'out of season' or of an exotic nature, as well as for reasons of lower purchase or cost price. Internationalization of supply of even indigenous products is common. The system developments needed to meet the demands for quality and consistency, including temperature control aspects, do impact on the channel composition. The handling systems to manage the air freighting of, for example, tomatoes from the Canary Islands, baby sweetcorn from Egypt or flowers from Malaysia require a considerable technological development. They also, however, represent a fundamental organizational and relationship shift.

As the number and range of temperature controlled products have increased, and a number of market failures have occurred, so the issue of food safety has become more central (Henson and Caswell, 1999; Kuznesof and Brennan, 2004). Failures of food safety in the UK (not all, of course, associated with failures of temperature control) are common on a localized and individual level. For example, there is a high level of personal food poisoning in the UK, although the extent to which this is a result of product or channel failure rather than an individual consumer's lack of knowledge or care is unclear. More publicly notable, however, have been national events ('food scares') such as listeria in cheese, salmonella in eggs and chickens, BSE in cattle and E coli 157 in meat. These national events raise concern and comment about food safety. There is thus a perception over the safety of supply of food and food chains, which in turn has focused attention on risk assessment and risk management. Temperature controlled supply chains gain importance therefore from the risks associated with failure and from the steps necessary to minimize these risks. Some of the steps are voluntary and company specific; others are required by legal developments over the last decade.

As a consequence of risk assessments and the major problems in food safety, temperature controlled supply chains have become a focal point for the development of food safety legislation across Europe. Although such legislation introduces requirements that cover a broad range of issues, one key aspect is the temperature conditions under which products are maintained. Such legislation, combined with increasing retailer liability to prosecution, has put great pressure on the standards of control throughout the food supply chain, particularly in the case of temperature control. For these reasons, temperature controlled supply chains are often seen as a specialist discipline within logistics. To some extent this is understandable, given the need for specialist facilities, eg warehouses, vehicles, refrigerators, etc to operate chilled or frozen distribution channels. This specialist market, however, is itself increasing in scale and scope, both as the market expands and as operational and managerial complexity increases.

The discussion above and comments in the introduction allow the identification of a number of key issues in temperature controlled supply chains. Here, three are identified for further discussion: the issues of costs, food safety and hazard analysis critical control points (HACCP), and partnerships.

As noted earlier, the integrity of temperature controlled supply chains is important for food safety. This places an obligation of care and duty of implementation on the supplier, retailer and logistics. In the UK, for example, the Food Safety Act of 1990 defined the storage, handling and transportation requirements for food products, including temperature control for certain categories. One of the requirements of the Food Safety Act 1990 makes it an absolute offence to sell food that is unfit for human consumption. Clearly, food that has 'gone off' due to inadequate temperature control can fall into this category. The Act, however, allows for a defence of 'due diligence' against any charges. Thus a business may be able to mount a defence based on evidence that all reasonable precautions had been exercised to avoid the commission of the offence. If we think about temperature control, then this implies that there needs to be a system of control maintenance, monitoring and recording (for evidence) of the temperature regimes in the supply chain.

The Food Standards (Temperature Control) Regulations of 1995 made it an offence to allow food to be kept at temperatures that could cause risk to health. This again implied a tightening of systems in the chain. This was effectively codified by the General Hygiene Act of 1995, which required all food businesses to adopt a risk management tool such as HACCP. Loader and Hobbs (1999) see this as a change in philosophy, representing a move away from an end product food safety inspection approach to a preventative, scientific focus with the responsibility for risk management placed on the food business proprietor. As a result, HACCP and other systems (Sterns, Codron and Reardon, 2001) have been vital to establish process controls through the identification of critical points in the process that need to be monitored and controlled (see the box below).

Hazard analysis critical control points (HACCP)

It is important in the application of the disciplines of an integrated temperature controlled supply chain to understand the principles of the obligations of suppliers, retailers and logistics service providers.

All have a duty of care for the product. In order to meet this duty of care they must demonstrate that they have applied due diligence in the structure and execution of their operation, ie that they have taken all reasonable methods to ensure the care of the product.

One of these reasonable methods is hazard analysis critical control points (HACCP), which is central to the discipline of chill chain integrity in logistics. The quality assurance department conduct a survey of the supply chain under their control with the objective of identifying those circumstances where the product might be exposed to unsuitable conditions, ie hazards. They rank these hazards according to the importance of their risk, eg high, medium, low. Procedures are then put in place at an appropriate level to prevent that risk.

So to express this differently: identify the hazards, analyse their importance, identify which are critical and set up control procedures at these points.

Once HACCP is put in place, it becomes a strong argument that due diligence is being practised.

For temperature controlled supply chains, there are big benefits from putting the physical and operational procedures in place along the whole length of the supply chain. This investment reduces a high risk to a low risk. By stabilizing the temperature throughout the life of the product, suppliers and retailers can concentrate on other aspects that can add value to the product, eg growing varieties.

Here is an example: the movement of chill goods from a DC to retail stores on a multi-temperature vehicle. Risk to food safety – high; risk of occurrence – high.

Critical control

- The temperature setting is stated on the load sheet and the run sheet.

- The loader checks the load sheet and sets the temperatures for the compartment.

- The loader secures the bulkhead.

- The loader switches the refrigeration on and ticks the relevant temperature on the load sheet.

- Once loading is complete, a supervisor checks the settings and switches against the load sheet and signs it off if it is correct.

- The load sheet is handed into the goods-out office.

- The driver checks the digital readings (usually at the front of the unit, visible in the rear-view mirror) against the load sheet. If they are correct, the driver signs off the load sheet and hands it in to the goods-out office.

- The goods-out clerk checks if the temperatures on the load sheet and the run sheet match and, if they are correct, allows the vehicle to leave.

- The goods-out supervisor does daily checks to assure compliance.

Source: Author interviews

The legislation in the UK was in essence a national response to approaches being recommended in Europe and codified in the EU legislation. The food scares in the UK of the late 1990s also brought forward a response. The Food Standards Act 1999 created the Food Standards Agency (FSA) in April 2000. The Act was intended to induce all those involved in the food supply chain to improve their food handling practices, including temperature control. There is no doubt that the FSA will continue to play a strong role in temperature controlled supply chains (http://www.foodstandards.gov.uk).

This onus of due diligence and the responsibility of businesses had a major effect on systems of control and monitoring of performance. It also, however, had an effect on the business relationships and governance in place. If a retailer, for example, wishes to be protected from claims, then it has to ensure that its suppliers are undertaking good practices, in addition to its own practice. This is true not only for retailer brand products, but for all sourced products. Because of this, traceability and tracking become more fundamental, and good partner-ships become crucial. As costs rise in introducing new systems, increasing the depth and quality of partnerships is a safeguard and it also offers possible cost benefits. As a result, partnerships expanded considerably post-1991 in the UK (Fearne and Hughes, 2000; Hughes, 1994; Loader and Hobbs, 1999; Wilson, 1996a, 1996b). Food retailers today are keen to have such partnerships and to use them in their marketing, as seen in the numerous 'farm assured' type schemes. Such partnerships and changes in organization of the supply chain are not restricted to UK suppliers. Dolan and Humphrey (2000) show how, in Africa, the requirements of the leading UK retailers have transformed the horticultural sector in scale and operational terms, leaving smaller producers in a precarious position. This scale dimension is linked closely to the legal requirements and the costs of compliance and potential chain failure.

However, it is not all cost and regulation, as there are operational and commercial benefits to be gained from proper temperature controlled supply chain management. These benefits might include an increase in shelf-life and freshness, better in-store presentation to the customer and thus better customer perception of products and the retailer. This increase in product quality and perception is the direct result of maintaining the correct temperature for that product group steadily and constantly throughout its supply chain journey. One major effect of an increase in shelf-life and freshness has been that consumers can notice the difference between product supplied through a fully temperature controlled supply chain and that supplied through a partially temperature controlled supply chain, and so make product and retailer choice decisions accordingly. Whilst it is generally the case today that the major food retailers maintain chill and cold chain integrity and thus have totally controlled temperature controlled supply chains, this has not always been the case. Temperature controlled supply chains have thus changed considerably over the last two decades.

The issues in temperature controlled supply chains outlined mainly in terms of the UK above are also found in other developed countries. The legislative position might be different but the net effect is the same. Such concerns are also spreading internationally for reasons considered in other contexts earlier. As points of production become more international, so the need to ensure consistency and safety is increased, particularly when production is occurring in developing and low-cost economies where the infrastructure may be less than anticipated. Similarly, as retailers internationalize their stores, so they need to ensure compliance in stores and supply chains in these other countries. In some cases they will use their investments in these areas to emphasize the quality and safety of their operations, including their food for sale. As consumers react to this, so the 'bar' for local retailers is raised. These issues are thus becoming more important in many countries.

Changes in temperature controlled supply chains

The temperature controlled supply chain has developed and changed since the 1980s. In the past in the UK, the supply chain consisted of single-temperature warehouses dedicated to narrow product ranges of food, eg butters, fats and cheeses at plus 5 degrees Celsius, dairy-based provisions, meat-based provisions, fresh meat and poultry, fruit and vegetables, and frozen products. The design, equipment and disciplines were only partially implemented so that there was incomplete integrity of the temperature control. Products were exposed to periods of high ambient temperature, which affected the shelf-life and the quality of the product. Single-temperature systems also meant that many more deliveries were needed. Such systems were essentially inefficient and ineffective.

Such a situation existed in the 1980s in Tesco (see Smith, 1998; Smith and Sparks, 1993, 2004; Sparks, 1986). In the mid-1980s, the Tesco temperature controlled supply chain consisted of a large number (27) of small single-temperature warehouses, each specializing in the storage, handling and delivery of a narrow product range. Examples of these sets of product ranges were: fresh produce; fresh meat and poultry; butters, fats and cheeses; chilled dairy provisions; chilled meat provisions; and frozen foods. Each set was managed by a different specialist logistics service provider organized on behalf of the manufacturer and supplier. The deliveries to the retail stores took place two or three times a week, with the temperature controlled vehicle going from one store to another delivering the appropriate number of pallets of products. The delivery notes and product checking were conducted at the back door of the store and the cost of delivery was included in the price of the product. Fresh meat and poultry was controlled on an individual case basis and charged by weight, as each case had a different weight (variable weight charging).

There are several limitations of this model of a temperature controlled supply chain. It was expensive to expand to meet large increases in overall growth in volume, as it required the building of more and more single-temperature warehouses. The retail delivery frequency was limited. The delivery volume drop size per store was small, and vehicles used were 'under-sized' because of problems over retail access. At that time there also was not full awareness of the importance of maintaining total integrity of the chill chain.

The strategy that Tesco decided upon was to build a small number (seven) of new large multi-temperature 'composite' warehouses that would store, handle and deliver the full range of product sets, all from the same location. The composite temperature regimes are: frozen at minus 25 degrees; cold chill at plus 1 degree; and exotic chill at plus 12 degrees. The manufacturers and suppliers of all the product sets make daily deliveries into the composite distribution centre. The composite delivery frequency to the retail stores increased to daily. The delivery vehicles had movable bulkheads and three temperature controlled evaporators so that up to three different temperature regimes could be set on the one vehicle (see Figure 3.3). The benefit was improved vehicle utilization and improved service to retail. Chill chain integrity disciplines were implemented rigorously from supplier to retail shelf.

There are other aspects to this change. Distribution and retail agreed a policy of not checking the goods at the retail back door, which improved the speed with which the goods could be transferred into the temperature controlled chambers at the store. This improved chill chain integrity. The goods were delivered in reusable plastic trays, on 'dollies' or on roll cages, which improved handling at store, in terms of both speed and quality (see Chapters 4 and 6). New store designs permitted the use of full-length vehicles, so improving efficiency.

Another major change in supply chains between the 1980s and 2000s has been the increasing pace of the order and replenishment cycle (McKinnon and Campbell, 1998). Today, with many fresh products, there is no stock held in the retail distribution centre overnight. Lead times have continued to be reduced. One of the key drivers of this increase in pace has been the development of information technology, which has enabled a large volume of data to be collected, processed and transmitted at faster speeds. Today data are collected from the point of sale and used in calculating future customer demand, which in turn forms the basis of the orders placed on suppliers. The scale, control and skill of the retail logistics operation has improved so that even distance-sourced products can be rapidly transported to their destinations at the regional distribution

Figure 3.3   *Multi-temperature vehicles* (source: *author photographs, 2001*)

Figure 3.3a   *Movable bulkheads*

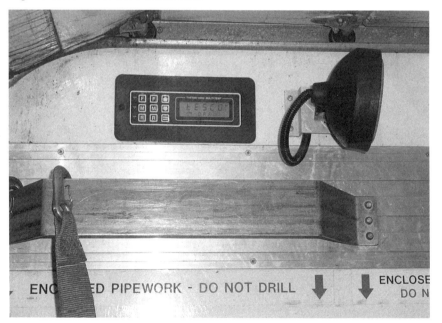

Figure 3.3b   *Compartment temperature setting*

centres. An example of this is the sourcing of produce from Spain direct from the growers into the distribution centres. These changes, encouraged by information technology amongst other factors, require changes in supply chain facilities and operations to ensure chill chain integrity.

Following the implementation of centralized distribution, attention turned to the condition of temperature controlled supply chains for the inbound product sets from the supplier and manufacturer into the regional distribution centres. The examination of the logistics of the inbound supply chain revealed that there were huge opportunities to improve transport efficiency. The increasing pace of the retail supply chain had resulted in most suppliers of temperature controlled product sets sending their vehicles long distances, but only partly filled, to the various retailers' regional distribution centres. So, for example, suppliers' vehicles carrying fruit and vegetables from a supplying region like Kent were following each other to distant regional distribution centres in Northern England and Wales, each with a partially full vehicle to the same destination. Clearly there was an opportunity for the consolidation of supply.

This process of consolidation saw the appointment of designated logistics service providers in the appropriate regions to manage and operate temperature controlled consolidation centres, accumulating full vehicle loads of temperature controlled products to despatch to the composite distribution centres. These consolidation centres also conducted quality assurance testing of the product. There were two benefits of placing the quality assurance function in the consolidation centres. The first was that they were close to the suppliers so that any problems could be dealt with face to face where required. The second benefit was that these vehicles did not then need to undergo quality assurance checking when they arrived at the distribution centre. This improved the turnaround time of the inbound vehicle, increasing its productivity and profitability, and also enabled the handling operation to commence earlier and so keep the goods in bay clear for the next set of deliveries. This was especially important in the early evening when a very high volume of produce harvested that same day is delivered.

Some of the effects of these changes to the Tesco supply chain are considered in Table 3.3. This summarizes the last 15–20 years of temperature control supply and the ways in which this has changed. Over the time period, the shelf-life for these products has increased considerably, and in the case of vegetables and top fruit it has

Table 3.3   Enhancements in shelf-life – Tesco

Stage	Soft Fruit	Top Fruit	Veg	Temperature Controlled Supply Chain Status and Improvement Action
Pre-1980				Single-temperature produce centres (three). Ambient and plus 5 degrees Celsius. Code dates not a legal requirement. Shelf-life managed at retail. Retail ordered from local suppliers without any technical support.
1980 to 1986				Two further produce centres. Operating procedures remained the same. Suppliers normally loaded in yard or from ambient bays. Many vehicles had curtain sides.
1986				Notice that code dates to become a legal requirement for produce. Produce technical team established shelf-life and introduced QC checks at distribution centres. 78-/48-hour ordering cycle to retail.
1987	2 CD + 2 CL = 4 days total	5 CD + 2 CL = 7 days total	3 CD + 2 CL = 5 days total	Code dates (CD) introduced for loose and pre-packed produce. In addition to the selling code dates there were additional days where product would be at its best. This time was called 'customer life' (CL). QC in produce depots to enforce specification. Two further produce centres. Code of practice introduced for suppliers included distribution centre controls and vehicle standards, eg no curtain-siders.
1989	2 CD + 4 CL = 6 days total	5 CD + 6 CL = 11 days total	3 CD + 5 CL = 8 days total	Six composite distribution centres opened. Separate temperature chambers of +3, +10, +15 for produce. Composite multi-temperature trailers deliver at +3 and +10 degrees Celsius, loading from sealed temperature controlled loading bays. Customer life extended by two days for soft fruit, four days for top fruit and three days for vegetables. No increase in code dates. Consumer demand for fruit and vegetables doubled as a consequence of the introduction of strict temperature control disciplines throughout the supply chain.
1990				Food Safety Act: to meet due diligence, hazard analysis critical control points (HACCP) introduced throughout the supply chain. The result was more consistent shelf-life but no increase in days. Retail stores only allowed to buy from suppliers with Technical approval.

Table 3.3   *continued*

Stage	Soft Fruit	Top Fruit	Veg	Temperature Controlled Supply Chain Status and Improvement Action
1995	2 CD + 5 CL = 7 days total	5 CD + 10 CL = 15 days total	3 CD + 6 CL = 9 days total	Produce temperature controlled consolidation hubs introduced. Six further hubs added over next three years. QA control introduced at hubs so quality checked before produce despatched to the composites. Hubs located close to supplier regions so prompt resolution of problems with supplier management. Shelf-life review showed increase of one day across all vegetables, soft fruit and stone fruit. Salads became inconsistent because of harvesting during the night before dew point. But there was a greater benefit of starting despatch earlier, especially from Spain. Retail order lead time 48/24 hours.
1997				Composite distribution centres changed produce chamber temperatures to +1 and +12 degrees Celsius with tighter variation of +/-1 degree from +/-2 degrees before. There was no change to shelf-life because the supply chain disciplines were fully in place.
1998	2 CD + 5 CL = 7 days total	6 CD + 10 CL = 16 days total	4 CD + 6 CL = 10 days total	Technical departments given targets to increase produce shelf-life. One potential improvement was to introduce US-type variety control. The benefit was only possible because of the very strict total supply chain temperature control. One extra day of code life for stores.
2000				Continuous replenishment introduced. The benefit was split deliveries into retail stores with different code dates for retail without any loss of customer life.
2002	2 CD + 5 CL = 7 days total	7 CD + 10 CL = 17 days total	5 CD + 6 CL = 11 days total	Further supply chain improvements in shelf-life to extend code dates by one day. No change to customer life to improve availability on selected lines, ie core vegetables, top fruit, stone fruit, but not salads or soft fruit. Three potential improvement methods: 1) atmospheric control, especially during the three-day delivery from Spain; 2) humidity control; 3) ethylene control.

Source: Author interviews

doubled (see Figure 3.4). This provides better product for longer for the consumer and is more efficient for the retailer. It does, as the table indicates, require a major reorientation of the supply chain and a dedication to standards. The overall effect however has been to provide fresher product more quickly and cheaply to the retail store and to lengthen the shelf life and quality time of a product for the consumer. Packaging logistics systems, through alterations to handling and packaging approaches, have an important role to play in this (see Chapter 4).

The discussion above is centred on developments in Tesco. Similar operations and developments have been introduced in other major food retailers. These have been needed to handle the massive expansion of demand in the temperature controlled sector in recent years and to compete with the market leader. Not all the changes and developments can be outlined above and in the tables. Changes to packaging, eg handling systems and transport environments, vacuum or other atmosphere controlled packaging, have also extended the shelf-life of products and improved in-store quality.

Our use of temperature controlled supply chains to illustrate in detail some of the aspects of concern in retail logistics shows the level of detail at which businesses operate. Systems have become so widespread and integrated, but complicated. Technology is a logical response to aspects of control, whether this is data capture or process monitoring. However, all aspects of the supply system have come under such scrutiny as retailers have used their increased power and expertise to work with manufacturers, suppliers and logistics services providers to improve the quality and consistency as well as capabilities of all food supply chains. Such alterations and approaches are

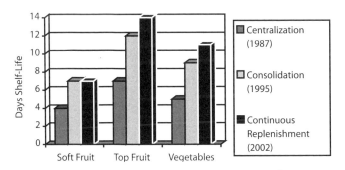

Figure 3.4   *Availability and shelf life in fresh food in Tesco 1987–2002*

going on across the world as the search for supply efficiency and effectiveness continues.

RETAILERS' LEADERSHIP OF LOGISTICS

This chapter has focused on aspects of change in retail logistics and temperature controlled supply chains. The emphasis has been placed on the extent and scale of change partly in response to the dimensions of retail change (Chapter 2) but most certainly led through the rising power of, and use of that power by, retailers. Across many countries and most retail sectors, retailers have increased in scale and power in relation to their suppliers and to manufacturers. In many areas of retail business, retailers have used this increased power to demand, structure and control change in operational practices. Retailers have taken over as the channel captains and have forced the pace of change in supply chains. As we have noted, there has been a restructuring of many aspects of retail supply systems as a consequence.

Some of these changes have effectively been 'ordered' by retailers. Manufacturers and suppliers have simply had to comply in order to maintain the business. The timing and presentation of suppliers into retailers' distribution centres are one example of this. However, the ability of retailers to order total change and the extent to which they can do so are constrained by the interdependence of retailers and their supply partners. Absolute power only works in some circumstances and for a certain period of time. Retailers have to continue working with suppliers and manufacturers, and thus adversarial relationships have only a limited ability to achieve supply chain objectives. Some of these changes have therefore been collaborative and channel transformative. The interdependence of food retailers and their suppliers leads to a search for potential benefits to all parties. Efficiencies in the supply chain are often produced by collaborative efforts rather than by undiscussed demands.

Such issues are most clear in the area of food and grocery handling systems and packaging. There are many choices to be made in this area but, by working together to produce effective systems and standards, joint benefits can be obtained. Standards such as handling systems and pack sizes, coding and reusable and returnable packaging systems provide channel-wide benefits. Alterations to the design and composition of packaging help at the store levels and in recycling as well as at all handling points in the channel. There are many such opportunities in food retailing logistics. The next chapter therefore considers the packaging choices to be made in the fresh food logistics system.

4   *Packaging and Fresh Food*

The discussion in the previous two chapters has focused on retail and logistics change. It has been noted that the ideas of supply chain management have been applied to improve the effectiveness and efficiency of retail supply chains. This has had implications for the administration of, and collaboration in, retail supply chains. The actual process of moving product, however, remains somewhat under-explored or under-explained in the descriptions and analysis thus far. There has been some mention of handling systems, and the idea of packaging logistics as one of the integrators in supply chain change has been raised. However, details have been limited.

This is not an unusual situation. An analysis of a recent selection of textbooks in the supply chain and logistics field (Table 4.1) shows that consideration of packaging and packaging logistics is uncommon. Indeed, of the eight UK or European books examined, only four contained any reference to packaging, and these were no more than a few pages in length and concentrated in three cases on the basic functions of packaging. This reinforces the literature searches by Johnsson (1998) and Saghir (2002), which found few articles that examined packaging from a logistics perspective. Indeed Johnsson (1998) noted that packaging was generally only discussed from a protection and

Table 4.1   Recent texts in logistics and their coverage of packaging

Text	Index and Coverage
Fernie and Sparks (2004)	Packaging and packaging waste, EU Directive (pp 22–23).
Bourlakis and Weightman (2004)	Packaging, new products (pp 157–60). Packaging and reverse logistics (pp 170, 226).
Christopher and Peck (2003)	–
Christopher (1998)	–
Grant *et al* (2006)	Packaging (pp 18, 277–81, 362–63).
Harrison and van Hoek (2002)	–
Kotzab and Bjerre (2005)	–
Waters (2003)	Packaging (pp 302–03).

palletization perspective. This lack of coverage is rather peculiar given the changes in this field that have enabled considerable advances in retail supply systems, particularly in fresh food. The implications from the earlier chapters are that consideration of packaging, as a logistics and supply chain integrator (the idea of packaging logistics), will bring considerable channel benefits. Packaging thus needs to move centre-stage.

This chapter therefore takes as its starting point the traditional ideas behind packaging. It presents a terminology of packaging and provides an introduction to the packaging industry. From this, developments in corrugated and plastics packaging and handling systems are·presented. Finally, the implications of these packaging changes for supply chains are drawn out to inform and illustrate the channel benefits of applying the disciplines of packaging logistics.

THE PURPOSES OF PACKAGING

'Packaging is a means of ensuring safe and efficient delivery of the goods in sound condition to the ultimate consumer, supplemented by efficient reuse of the packaging or recovery and/or disposal of the packaging material at minimum cost' (based on Paine (1981), used by Bjärnemo, Jönson and Johnsson, 2000).

Before considering the purposes of packaging in more detail, we need to classify the different types or levels of packaging. There are three levels of packaging normally considered, primary, secondary and tertiary packaging (see Figure 4.1). Primary packages hold the basic product and are brought home from the shop by the end consumer. Secondary packages, or transport packages, are designed to contain several primary packages. A secondary package could be taken home by the end consumer or be used by retailers as an aid when loading shelves in the store. The third level of packaging, tertiary packages, comes into use when a number of primary or secondary packages are assembled as, for example, on a pallet. Examples of tertiary packaging are stretch films, tension nets or ties for strapping the unit load. It has

The package life cycle

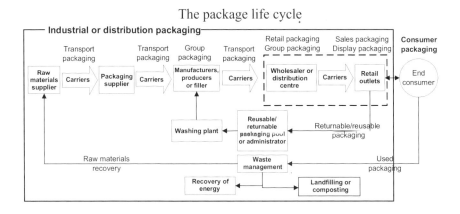

The levels of the packaging system

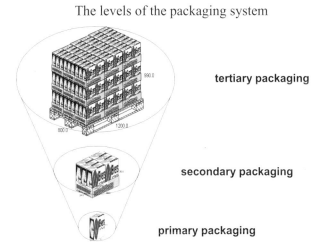

Source: Saghir (2004)

Figure 4.1   *Different packaging terms used and the levels of the packaging system*

to be recognized that this classification can be made more complex by the use of various descriptors and interchangeable terms. Table 4.2 provides a listing and definition of some of the common terms in use and relates these to the three levels presented above. It is also clear that these three levels of packaging operate in different ways within the product life cycle (see Figure 4.1).

Table 4.2   Definition of different packaging types

Packaging Type	Definition
Primary packaging	Packaging that is in contact with the product. The packaging that the consumer usually takes home.
Consumer packaging	Same as primary packaging.
Sales packaging	Same as consumer packaging.
Secondary packaging	Secondary packaging is designed to contain several primary packages.
Box	Often a secondary packaging. Same as transport packaging.
Transport packaging	Packaging that is devised to facilitate handling, transport and storage of a number of primary packages in order to provide efficient production and distribution as well as prevent physical handling and transport damage.
Industrial packaging	Same as transport packaging.
Bulk packaging	Same as transport packaging, but greater than 1 cubic metre.
Container	Same as transport packaging.
Distribution packaging	Same as transport packaging.
Grouping (or tertiary) packaging	Packaging that is devised to facilitate the protection, display, handling and/or transport of a number of primary or transport packages.
Display packaging	Same as grouping packaging, quite often with an emphasis on display features.
Retail packaging	Same as grouping packaging, with a special emphasis on the design to fit in the store shelf.
Used packaging	Packaging/packaging material remaining after the removal of the product it contained.
Waste packaging	Same as used packaging, but less and less of it as packaging is not wasted, but recovered.

Source: Saghir (2002)

As Figure 4.1 shows, packages, when they are stacked together, are traditionally placed on wooden pallets. Pallets are normally of a standard size footprint, which in Europe is 1,200 millimetres by 800 millimetres or 1,200 millimetres by 1,000 millimetres (the latter is the normal standard used in the UK). There is also a half-size pallet, 800 millimetres by 600 millimetres, and even a quarter-size pallet, 600 millimetres by 400 millimetres. The concept of the pallet as both packaging and standardization mechanism is of key importance to developing ideas about packaging logistics.

The distinction between packaging and the distribution system is not strictly defined. A practical approach is to say that transport vehicles, for example bulk transport vehicles, that contain products without further packaging are not regarded as packaging, as their main function is to move the goods and not solely to provide protection. It can be complicated, however, as for example with the pallet. The pallet is a means for the packaging development team to optimize the protection and movement of products. Using the same reasoning for pallets as for vehicles would mean that the pallet is part of the system to protect the product, but also part of the distribution system, as it is there to aid handling, storage and movement.

As might be anticipated from Figure 4.1, there are different purposes and functions of packaging, depending on the type and role of the packaging involved and its place in the distribution channel. Figure 4.2 attempts to provide a guide to the most important functions of packaging at different levels. The main levels of protection, performance and information are then subdivided into further functions. These would be recognizable to most involved in logistics systems. The figure also attempts to examine the drivers influencing packaging (seen in Chapters 2 and 3) and the benefits deriving from packaging. Within the figure it is clear that many elements of the performance component and of the benefits have direct impacts on logistics and supply chains. These are the focus here. Before considering these opportunities, however, the packaging industry itself needs introduction.

THE PACKAGING INDUSTRY: STRUCTURE AND DYNAMICS

Packaging is a trade of great importance to the industrialized world. It has seen tremendous growth since the 1950s. Packaging is normally one

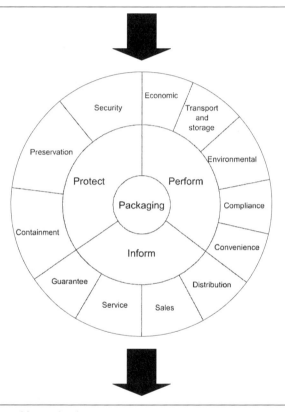

Source: Pira/University of Brighton (2004)

Figure 4.2   *The functions of packaging*

of the 10 largest industries in a country, responsible for 1–2 per cent of the GNP. Packaging has become an integrated part of the development of society and has grown with new infrastructures, new distribution concepts and changing demographics (Pira/University of Brighton, 2004). According to industry sources (www.packaging-gateway.com, accessed 26 October 2005), the global packaging industry is worth US $424 billion, and this is expected to grow over the next decade by over 3.5 per cent per annum. The European market is the most significant geographical market (30 per cent), but is closely followed by North America (28 per cent) and Asia (27 per cent). Paper (corrugated) remains the largest material used (36 per cent), but plastic (34 per cent), metal (17 per cent) and glass (10 per cent) are also significant. Plastic has been gaining ground on paper-based packaging in recent years. In terms of sectors, the food industry dominates (38 per cent), with beverages (18 per cent), pharmaceuticals (5 per cent) and cosmetics (3 per cent) also of importance. The spread of sectors that require some form of packaging is well marked by the 36 per cent of the total market that is found in sectors beyond these 'big four'.

Corrugated packaging

The corrugated board industry has been very successful over many decades, and has developed strongly with the industrial production of consumer goods in Europe. The market continues to grow. During the 1990s it more than doubled in size, although demand varied enormously amongst countries and regions. Traditionally, corrugated paper has been the largest single component of packaging consumption, usually with a share of 40 per cent of the packaging materials by weight. Some 40 per cent of the corrugated packaging is used by the food and beverage industries. Corrugated board packaging use is expected to continue to grow for general fast-moving consumer goods but for fresh foods the trend is slowing down, although the most commonly used transport packaging material for fresh food is corrugated (63 per cent) (FEFCO, 2003).

The corrugated board companies have met challenges in their market by cooperating, merging and rationalizing. They have developed their products and markets by investing in production equipment, packaging design and tailor-made services that meet the needs of their customers. The industry has had to adapt to succeed and retain its dominant position in packaging solutions. These companies have also combined the production of paper and packaging to satisfy market requirements.

This has been important for large customers that operate in several different countries and have required their suppliers to specialize in providing particular types of materials and packaging to all their outlets. Through this integration it has been possible to serve the larger customers with standardized materials, specialist designs and customized services for all the locations in their various countries of operation.

The geographical structure of the corrugated board industry is such that the production is decentralized because the material is bulky; to remain competitive the transport range is best limited to 200 kilometres. The packaging research and development function is usually located at the centre, while the production remains local to the customers. These local production plants (known as converters) also have designers, who can make adjustments to meet the local needs. In the case of large customers with specialist requirements, it is possible to produce the same type of material and package in all the plants and still make special adjustments if needed for the local customers.

Alongside these large companies there are also manufacturers that provide sheet corrugated paper production and converting capacity at the local or national level. These manufacturers offer a special service of individual package designs or standard packages that are made available whenever the customer needs them. This structure and organization give the whole industry a flexibility that is one of the reasons why it has been so successful. Figure 4.3 shows some corrugated packaging use in fresh food retailing, both in a retail and in a distribution setting.

Plastic packaging

The plastics era started in the 1920s, with thermoset plastics, providing the initial applications for the need to insulate electrical devices, which was necessary for the safe handling and distribution of electric power. From the 1930s, new types of thermoplastic polymers were developed, resulting in the first plastic bags. Pouches made of low density polyethylene (LDPE) were introduced during the 1950s. These plastic bags formed an important component in the introduction of the concept of deep-freezing technology for food. Later on, plastic packaging as primary packaging enabled the food industry to offer consumers higher-quality products with a longer shelf-life, based on the high-technology development of multi-layer laminates, vacuum-packing and modified atmosphere packaging.

Figure 4.3   *Corrugated packaging in fresh food retailing*

Figure 4.3a   *Retail display in the UK* (source: *author photograph, 2005*)

Figure 4.3b   *Distribution handling, Italy* (source: *author photograph, 2001*)

At the beginning of the 1960s, high density polyethylene (HDPE) was introduced as a commodity plastic raw material. This material has good production properties, is easy to handle and does not need much additives, except colouring and an additive providing resistance to the radiation from sunlight (UV). It is 100 per cent recyclable. Trials show that an HDPE polymer can be reused over five product life cycles during 50 years before the polymer loses its properties and the energy content is finally utilized. This forms the basis for the argument proving that it is sustainable for a large and growing industry to use raw materials that are still based on fossil resources. Natural gas, methane, and excess gas from oil refineries are today the main sources for the production of thermoplastics. It is also fully possible to produce HPDE from biogas or other renewable raw materials sources, although prices are still too high to attract real demand for the market.

In parallel with the process development of HDPE as a raw material, the technology of injection moulding production was developed. This allowed manufacturers to focus on their production productivity per hour. In terms of the investment calculation in the plastic industry, the cost of the injection moulding machines and their individual moulds and tools still accounts for the largest part of the product cost. This is further strongly influenced by the actual price for the raw material, which over the years has been very volatile. Today, most of the packaging production is automated, and must be operated on a 24-hour, seven-day-a-week basis to achieve the profit level desired.

Beverage crates

At the end of the 1950s, the plastic revolution within food packaging and distribution started the development of new types of secondary and tertiary packaging. The beverage industry was the first to adopt these new products, followed by the meat-handling sector and bakeries. More hygienic and ergonomically better packaging, in HDPE, replaced wooden beverage crates and steel containers. From the outset, these products were designed for reuse in company-internal systems or closed-loop systems circulating from suppliers to retailers. Beverage crates form the only returnable transport packaging system where end consumers are involved. The long life cycle of the first beverage crates in Sweden is striking. When the 25-bottle crates from the 1960s were replaced by a more ergonomic 20-bottle crate in the late 1980s, surprisingly many of the oldest crates were delivered into the national take-back campaign, where old bottle crates were fragmented into small chips in mobile mills and classified as first-class recycling material for injection moulding, in spite of more than 20 years of use in its first life cycle.

During the 1990s, new polymer-based materials were introduced, providing the basis for a revolution within all industry sectors, including food packaging. Polypropylene (PP), another thermoplastic material, was developed further to withstand the temperature stresses on plastic crates and trays. These must keep their dimensions and mechanical properties within the range from +40 degrees C to −30 degrees C. PP is now becoming the leading material in new systems for reusable plastic crates and trays. Just like HDPE, PP is 100 per cent recyclable, and only colouring and UV-protection additives are needed.

As noted above, plastic packaging accounted for 34 per cent of all packaging in 2004 (www.packaging-gateway.com). Primary packaging accounts for the large majority of all plastics packaging used by consumers and industry. Polyethylene (PE) dominates the packaging market, accounting for 56 per cent by weight of all packaging produced by processors. Five other plastics – polypropylene (PP), polyethylene terephthalate (PET), polystyrene (PS), polyvinyl chloride (PVC) and expanded polystyrene (EPS) cover most of the remaining 44 per cent. The dominant material is low density polyethylene (LDPE and LLDPE) for plastic bags and foils, eg shrink film, followed by high density polyethylene (HDPE) and polypropylene (PP).

Traditionally, the plastics industry had been based on a large number of small or medium-sized family-owned companies, operating for a regional or national market. However, increases in raw material costs, lower profit margins and lower-cost competition from other European countries as well as from the developing countries, together with the need for new investment in expensive high-tech equipment to achieve better productivity and higher profit margins, have all triggered a massive consolidation within the plastic packaging industry. In addition, the major customer groups, such as the mechanical and automotive industries, have become global and require packaging suppliers to have the capacity to cover whole continents. Today there are fewer than 10 major suppliers of secondary and tertiary packaging for the food sector. These suppliers dominate the European market and they have the power to drive forward the product innovation and concept design development.

Plastic trays

During the 1960s a large number of small, family-owned plastic manufacturers started production of different types of plastic trays for local or national markets. No standards were available, resulting in a multitude of different sizes and 'footprints' and handling difficulties when stacking the different types of trays with each other. Within the automotive industry this problem was identified earlier than in the food sector. European standards (CEN) for automotive packaging were developed during the 1980s, followed during the 1990s by national and European standards for different types of trays within the food sector. Returnable plastic trays accounted for over 31 per cent of fresh food retail sales in Europe in 2003 (FEFCO, 2003).

The reasons why food sector stakeholders choose plastic trays are mainly based on economics, hygiene and ergonomics. In those situations where there are short- or medium-haul distribution distances, together with the demand for high hygienic standards, workplace safety and good ergonomics, as well as cost efficiency, it makes good business sense to choose reusable HDPE or PP packaging. Linpac, one of the largest suppliers in Europe of plastic crates, trays and pallets, has summarized the main arguments for reusable returnable packaging (www.linpac.com, 2003):

The use of [reusable] returnable transit equipment continues to increase as our customers seek to reduce their reliance on one trip packaging and the associated waste recovery and recycling costs. The advantages of returnable systems continue to stack up:

- Improved product protection.

- Better temperature control.

- Standardization of outer [dimensions] enables more efficient use of pallet and vehicle space.

- Elimination of need for packaging assembly increases operating productivity.

- Primary packaging reductions and cost savings.

- Packaging waste reduction.

- Benefits of using plastic transit container as merchandising unit in terms of product presentation and speed of loading onto shelf.

The increasing interest in reusable packaging is demonstrated in the statistics provided by the Association of Plastic Manufacturers in

Europe (APME, www.apme.org). In 1992, 36 million plastic trays were reused in Western Europe. This figure increased to 84 million in 1998 and reached over 150 million by 2003. This means an increase of 80 per cent in only five years. In Sweden, Svenska Retursystem AB, the company for returnable trays and pallets for the food sector, had quite a slow start during 2000 and 2001, but has now grown from 11 million circulations during 2002 to an estimated 62 million in 2005 (Svenska Retursystem, www.retursystem.se).

Figure 4.4 illustrates some plastic tray and box systems in fresh food retailing, including in retail and distribution settings. The figure also illustrates some of the large range of sizes, shapes and functions to which plastic packaging can be put and the ability of such packaging to be stacked before and after transportation/use.

RETURNABLE PACKAGING

The discussion above points to an important component of packaging, namely its reuse in the supply chain. When one looks at many retail stores, there are many packaging components that are simply thrown away or at best collected for recycling (see Figure 4.3). But there are also components that are collected for reuse in the system. The pallet is one example, but there are others, as the growth in plastic packaging suggests (Figure 4.4 illustrates some examples). These returnable and reusable elements are the focus of this book. As is immediately apparent, with pressures to work at a supply chain level, there are important decisions to be made over standards and specifications for all packaging, but especially returnable systems, across those involved in the supply chain. As a starting point it is important to ensure that the terminology in this area is understood (see Gustafsson, 2005).

The different types of transport packaging that can be returned for reuse are defined as *returnable* packaging. *Reusable* packaging is another definition commonly used as the opposite of one-way packaging. The reuse can take place in-house, in the same or in another supply chain, for the same or for any other type of products. *Recyclable* packaging is a definition of the possibility of recovering the *material* of the packaging for reuse as new packaging material or as raw material for other products.

Figure 4.4   *Plastic packaging in fresh food retailing*

Figure 4.4a   *Asda potato boxes* (source: *author photograph, 2005)*

Figure 4.4b   *Jersey milk* (source: *author photograph, 2005)*

Figure 4.4c   *Aerated crates, Italy* (source: *author photograph, 2001)*

Figure 4.4d
Collapsibility of empty plastic trays (source: *author photograph, 2001)*

Figure 4.4e   *Plastic trays in retail display in the Netherlands* (source: *author photograph, 2005)*

Trays, boxes, totes, crates, pallets and pallet containers

Returnable transport packaging includes the items discussed in the following sections.

Trays, boxes, totes and crates

The common footprint is 600 millimetres by 400 millimetres or 400 millimetres by 300 millimetres, and the height varies according to product and filling requirements. Trays, boxes and totes can have lids, separate or attached to the box.

Trays, boxes, totes and crates can be *stackable*, ie they can be stacked in such a way that the top design fits with the bottom design of the boxes to be put on top of each other. The design also secures the stack from collapsing. Maximum stacking height varies, but working safety regulations within the European Union recommend a maximum stacking height of 1.20 metres. This results in loading efficiency; if two pallet loads, each 1.20 metres high, are stacked on each other, the loading capacity of a trailer or a container is fully utilized (provided that the maximum weight limit is not exceeded).

Boxes can also be *stack- and nestable*. The nestable function is a common requirement in all returnable packaging systems, as this allows for space reduction when transporting empty packaging back for cleaning and refilling. The stack and nest function influences the volume capacity of the box, since the rigid walls cannot be 90 degrees in relation to the bottom of the box. Instead, the box is designed to have a sloping sides configuration to allow nesting. The nestable function can be acquired in two common ways: *180-degree rotation* of a sloping sided box, or a *swingbar/bale arm* construction on a sloping sided box where the swingbar/bale arm works as support for the box above in a stack. Swingbars/bale arms are easily folded up when the packaging is empty, thus allowing a nesting capacity of up to approximately 75 per cent, ie four empty boxes will take up the same loading height as one filled box. The empty nesting capacity is then defined as 1:4.

Interstackability is a requirement in focus within food distribution, ie different types of returnable boxes as well as one-way boxes can be stacked together with the same security as if there were only one type of transport packaging in the stack. Stackable boxes normally have vertical (90 degree) rigid walls. However, interstackability can also be obtained with boxes with sloping sides.

The third type of returnable box is the *foldable* or *collapsible* box. The walls of the box can be folded down, thus resulting in a maximum reduction of space needed for empty packaging. This type of box allows maximum inside volume for optimal space utilization. The drawback is the need for more physical handling when raising and collapsing this type of packaging. This form is expanding in use.

Trays, boxes, totes and crates in returnable systems are normally made of thermoplastics, HDPE or PP. It is also possible to find systems where trays, boxes or crates are made of wood, plywood, often metal-enforced, steel or cardboard of such quality that transport packaging items can be reused.

Bottle trays

As glass beverage bottles are successively phased out, being replaced with reusable or one-way PET bottles, there is no longer any need for heavy-duty beverage crates. Instead, a special type of tray is introduced, thus enhancing logistics efficiency. This tray forms a self-supported pallet load, with no need for filming or strapping. If one-way PET bottles are used, empty trays can be nested into each other, thus reducing return transport space capacity by more than 50 per cent. As this type of tray is not in direct contact with food, it is possible to use recycled plastic raw material from old, ground-up bottle crates as raw material for the production of bottle trays. This type of returnable transport packaging for beverages may very well be used by other business sectors where products are filled and delivered in bottles.

Pallets

These are normally of standard-size footprint EUR 1,200 millimetres by 800 millimetres or 1,200 millimetres by 1,000 millimetres. There is also a half-size pallet of 800 millimetres by 600 millimetres. Even a quarter-size pallet of 600 millimetres by 400 millimetres is in use in many European countries. Returnable pallets can be made of wood in accordance with European and/or national standard requirements for returnable wooden pallets. Returnable pallets can also be made of thermoplastics, normally HDPE or PP, which also meets European and/or national standard requirements concerning temperature stability, dynamic and static loading capacity, etc.

Pallet containers

These normally have the same footprint standards as full-size pallets, but are equipped with rigid or foldable walls. The use of pallet containers reduces the need for primary packaging of the products, thanks to the protective strength of the pallet container. Pallet containers are usually made of metal-enforced plywood or thermoplastics. Plastic returnable pallets and pallet containers may be equipped with in-mould radio frequency identification (RFiD) chips. This technology offers the users of returnable pallets and pallet containers many types of advantages (see Chapter 9).

Common types of applications for returnable transport packaging

Returnable transport packaging can be designed for single-product use, multi-product use, single-loop pool systems (one company to one company: from company A to company B and then back to company A again, etc), multi-loop pool systems (from one company to many companies and then back to the filler again, etc) and open-loop pool systems (multi-user, multi-product).

Single-product use

This type of returnable transport packaging is designed to carry and protect just one type of product or a family of products with similar physical dimensional requirements concerning footprint size and height. Single-product returnable packaging is most common in single-loop systems, but it can also be found as a packaging unit used in multi-loop systems, eg bread trays.

Multi-product use

Returnable transport packaging designed to carry and protect many different types of products must meet a longer list of requirements. Often the result is a compromise. One example of a compromise is to decide if the packaging, in this case a tray, should be ventilated or not. Certain products require ventilation in order to keep their freshness, while other types of products must be kept in a completely closed storage to avoid contamination from outside or to prevent the risk of liquids leaking from carried products, which may contaminate the outside.

Single-loop pool system

This is the most simple and non-complex type of returnable packaging pool system. The supplier/filler delivers its products in returnable transport packaging, such as trays, pallet containers and/or pallets, to one customer. When emptied, the returnable transport packaging items are sent back to the filler again. This type of packaging can be either for single-product or for multi-product use. In purchasing transport services, the supplier needs to negotiate return transport services from the customer to get the returnable packaging items back again. Normally this type of take-back transport can be obtained at a favourable cost by using imbalances in the transport system and by allowing the transport company to take back empty transport packaging during non-rush hours.

Multi-loop pool system

In a multi-loop pool system, one supplier/filler delivers its products in returnable transport packaging, such as trays, pallet containers and/or pallets, to several customers. In a multi-loop pool system, the requirements placed on logistics skills increase. In order to control and get the returnable packaging items back from all customers, the supplier/filler must design an administrative system that, by using certain tools, encourages the customers to send empty packaging back. Such tools can be deposit systems, or systems where the customer is invoiced a fee per day or per week for employing returnable packaging in its operations. Also, in a multi-loop pool system, the supplier/ filler must negotiate return transport services. At this stage of complexity many suppliers/fillers start to consider third-party solutions to get rid of all the work caused by ordering return transport services, checking and tracking where empty packaging is located, invoicing customers, etc.

Open-loop pool system

This is the most complex logistics system for returnable transport packaging. But it is also the system level where both large and small companies can be members on equal conditions. There are two common ways to run an open-loop pool system.

The first way is for a group of companies (normally along a supply chain) to identify a general need for returnable packaging. They form a membership organization, which in turn opens a separate non-profit pool company, which is the legal owner of all returnable packaging items. The members/owners of the pool company provide the financing tools required to invest in returnable packaging. The main task of the pool company is to operate the pool system, establish a control system, design the administration and – if needed – operate or manage a washing and maintenance facility. The non-profit pool company is operated with full transparency for the members.

The second way is for a third-party, commercial logistics services provider to offer returnable transport packaging items to many types of companies, some of which are in a supply chain, some not. The availability issue is one of the most important aspects. The third-party company guarantees that each customer with a need for returnable transport packaging will be supplied in accordance with its needs. The user of returnable transport packaging is invoiced a fixed fee per item usage. The third-party company is responsible for arranging return transports, and for cleaning and maintenance.

The difference between the two types in operating an open-loop pool system is the cost for using returnable packaging. Members of non-profit pool companies argue that they have a lower cost per used item, that they have an overall view of the system's functionality and that they are empowered to improve the system over time. When arguing for a member-owned pool company, the indirect costs for human resource input must be taken into consideration. Members must be interested in taking an active part in the planning and execution of the operations, and must see the commercial advantages of having access to full visibility and transparency that a member-owned pool company provides.

When arguing for a third-party solution, on the other hand, a company may see the advantage of not being forced to get involved in the management and physical operations of a pool system. There is a certain level of convenience to be achieved, naturally depending on the reliability of the third-party service provider. One reason for companies *not* to use third-party service providers is fear of the nightmare events that may occur if the service provider cannot keep its promises and a supplier suddenly has no packaging available for their products.

Why do companies choose returnable packaging?

The overall dominating primary reason for actors in business-to-business distribution to introduce returnable transport packaging systems is the potential of total cost savings. When simple calculations show that the pay-off time for a system with returnable transport packaging can be one to three years, the parties involved may see the opportunity of creating cost savings. These calculations include costs for purchasing one-way packaging or fees for use of externally owned pallets compared with year-based costs per trip use of returnable transport packaging. The uncertainty factor in this calculation is estimating the number of trips per year. The higher the speed of circulation and the number of trips, the better the economy is. The problem, however, is having to estimate the circulation speed in advance and identify what parameters may endanger and reduce the circulation speed.

If the parties involved try to include more logistics parameters in their calculations in order to get a more precise comparison, there will be a better basis for decisions, but some uncertainty will remain depending on the difficulty of predicting the overall performance of the planned returnable transport packaging system. This uncertainty can be remedied by suppliers of returnable transport packaging, who can provide valuable advice by using their extensive experience of packaging pool systems' performance in existing systems in operation within the actual business sector.

The loss ratio is the second most important parameter that may jeopardize the success of a returnable transport packaging system. How should the system be designed to minimize loss due to theft or non-authorized use? (Non-authorized means returnable transport packaging being used for purposes not included in the pool system set-up.) A deposit system may be one measure in order to prevent losses in business-to-business pool systems, especially if it is a multi-party pool system. The introduction of tags or in-mould equipment, such as microchips or RFiD (radio frequency identification devices), may prevent unauthorized use or theft (see Chapter 9).

Finding ways to reduce the amount of damaged products can be another main driving force in certain business sectors. Normally, returnable transport packaging is tougher and provides better protection against shock than one-way packaging (of course, one-way packaging can offer enough product protection as well, but usually that would require more packaging material at a higher price, which may cause an increased waste handling problem at the customer's production sites).

Since returnable transport packaging has such protection properties, there is a potential for certain suppliers to skip primary packaging and thus save money and time. There will also be a time saving potential for the customer, when delivered products do not need to be unwrapped before being put onto retail display.

Costs for waste handling can be the third driving force. Every minute or second that can be saved in handling workforce costs is worth a lot in many business sectors. Normally, the handling of returnable packaging requires less input of manual work than the handling of empty one-way packaging. This parameter is, however, much discussed from different perspectives and not valid in many cases.

Space reduction of empty packaging items, especially trays, is a key success parameter. If the actors can use collapsible trays, cost savings can be achieved as compared with return transports of rigid-wall trays. There is also an environmental aspect, namely that the need for emission-causing transports must be kept at a minimum.

GENERAL PACKAGING PRINCIPLES

Nowadays there is a general awareness of the increase in concern about environmental issues and the repercussions of environmental waste legislation in Europe. The reasons justifying the need to change how packaging is designed and used are generally understood. But aside from these environmental pressures to change the thinking about packaging, the industry has taken steps of its own to develop a set of criteria for good packaging design. An assessment of the developments from those earlier stages, in both the corrugated and the plastic packaging industry, can lead on to an evaluation of their strengths and weaknesses. Those earlier conditions gave rise to the traditional definition of packaging, given earlier (Bjärnemo, Jönson and Johnsson, 2000; Paine and Paine, 1983), which sets the scene for an examination of the current criteria for good box design.

Historically, packaging has mainly been evaluated by considering its basic functions, eg from chemical, mechanical and biological points of view (Saghir and Jönson, 2001). These definitions are functional, with the design criteria set by a single company, usually the product manufacturer. The designs incorporated the assessment by that particular company of the needs for the product's protection as it travelled to its intended destination.

Although, over time, the industry has evolved from small family businesses to large corporate organizations, these companies have usually worked independently and separately. There is little evidence of joint and collaborative effort with other parties in the supply chain, in which those companies involved actively cooperated to enhance and drive forward the development of packaging (Saghir, 2004). For this reason, the traditional point of view does not address the multifunctional nature of packaging.

There were some important consequences of this isolated packaging manufacturer design perspective and method of working. For example, there were no standard grades of corrugated board in the whole of Europe. Many countries used the weight or grammage of corrugated board as the sole criterion to describe the material. Some packaging suppliers judged that their own specific design of tailor-made packaging for individual products would function more efficiently for their own logistics operations than would design standardization criteria accepted from 'outside'. This type of approach by some packaging suppliers meant that they did not learn from looking further downstream into the handling operations within retail distribution. Such independently designed packaging solutions created much trouble in their handling along the retail supply chain. This resulted in damage to product quality and the subsequent loss of customer business at retail. It is this type of issue that has stimulated the development of a broader set of criteria for good box design.

Criteria for good packaging design

There have been several changes in thinking about the various purposes of packaging design. As a consequence, packaging design has now gone beyond the demands placed on it by basic packaging performance (protection, facilitation of distribution and information). As has been seen, there are different purposes and functions of packaging depending on the type and role of the packaging involved together with its place in the distribution channel and in the life cycle of a package (see Figure 4.1).

Figure 4.2 provided a guide to the most important functions of packaging at the different levels. New aspects are growing in importance, and new concepts in packaging systems provide opportunities to match the requirements of new lifestyles arising from the demands of changing demographics such as the increased number of small families and an older population (Pira/University of Brighton, 2004). These demographic trends, together with the need for traceability of products, require packaging solutions that ensure both product safety and supply chain efficiency.

Good packaging specification includes the technical aspects of graphic design of the brand and marketing information with the need to provide the product information, within the legislative framework. This is an aspect that is very visible to the consumer at the point of retail display (as seen in Chapter 2). The interaction of packaging material with the product is also important. Examples are dyes in printing ink that might migrate into the product (ie through back-printing via the rollers), or ingredients like tomato that might corrode certain materials, or peel oil in citrus fruits and certain aromas that might migrate into plastics.

Efficient unit load theory is an important contribution to the criteria for good packaging design because the unit load is an aspect of the interface between the packaging and the distribution systems. The focus is on the benefits of a small family of modular and compatible standardized packages, eg box or pallet sizes (as seen in Figure 4.1). Such standard dimensions make it possible to use standard handling equipment, eg forklifts for handling and standard pallet racks for storage. In addition, efficient unit loads make it possible to optimize the space utilization within transport vehicles. When looking at the 'cube', trailer and truck space can be used more efficiently, thus meeting demands for a lower environmental impact from transport. Several reports show that there is at least a 15 per cent improvement potential by better space utilization in vehicles (Department of Transport, 2003; DLF, 1990; Swahn and Söderberg, 1992). The advantages of applying efficient unit loads are obvious and well recognized.

The environmental debate and legislation

Good packaging criteria help to achieve the packaging purpose of increasing efficiency in supply chain systems and so add value to a country's economy. It is important to select solutions that not only give a proper performance but also use the minimum of resources in order to keep the environmental impact as low as possible. This has also been driven by the environmental legislation.

The environmental legislation (eg Packaging and Packaging Waste Directive 1996, Directive 94/62/EG, 1994 OT L 365) has motivated the packaging industry to adapt and change. The industry has successfully decreased the material weight in both consumer and transport packaging through packaging design and material development. This environmental pressure is likely to accelerate in future years, and the packaging industry will come under increasing pressure to respond. This pressure will be to reduce the amount of packaging needed in the supply system. There are four main avenues that can be followed to achieve this objective: recovery, reuse, recycling and dematerialization. Only after these opportunities have been exhausted should waste be sent for disposal in a landfill site, for which there is a charge. However, after 1 January 2005, the option of sending waste to landfill has been further restricted, since the EU Waste Directive aims at minimizing the landfill waste volumes.

The Packaging and Packaging Waste Directive allows member states within the EU to 'encourage reuse systems for packaging, which can be reused in an environmentally sound manner, provided they do not conflict with the EU Treaty'. This environmental debate has created discussion about the benefits of using either one-way transport packaging made of corrugated board or plastic trays that can be reused many times. This debate has caused some confrontation between the respective packaging manufacturing companies. The points at issue include the logistics of supply, hygiene, costs, efficiency, image and standards. The balance between the different materials used has changed, and in 2004 corrugated board packaging decreased to around 40 per cent of the market, while returnable plastic trays rose to 40 per cent (of which almost 80 per cent are used for fresh food) and wooden trays remained at just under 20 per cent (FEFCO, 2003).

Industry responses to design and environmental issues

The corrugated board industry designs packaging that is adapted not only to every shape and size of product but also to the different types of distribution systems. Through this flexibility in design, the industry believes that the resulting transport and warehouse cubic efficiency is very good, because no volume is wasted, as the packaging is designed to fit tightly around the product it is protecting. When this is combined with stacking the packages on to different types of distribution units such as pallets, cages or other unit loads, there is a very efficient use of the available transport cubic volume (Figure 4.3b is an example). These unit loads are also efficient when the product is being handled at the retail store.

There is a widespread use of modern computer-aided design tools that make it possible for the local plants to exchange information with each other and get ideas about what designs have worked for specific products and what materials are suitable for the different distribution systems. This means that it is not only the large customers that get access to future industrial development resources, but also the small local customers, as the central development is passed on to the local regions and markets. The application of packaging performance criteria is becoming more critical as the efficient use of the material and the management of the production resource increases in importance. Through the application of these performance specifications it is possible to establish what strength of properties the packaging needs to have. These strengths of properties are described through different corrugated board material properties. In addition to the material speci-fications, the corrugated board industry has established standard pack-aging types. They are divided into three types, regular slotted containers (RSC), trays and wrap-arounds. Within each group there are a number of alternative standard designs. A designer therefore often starts with a standard design and makes adjustments in this depending on demand. By using the standard designs as the basis, it is easy to communicate between different plants. Besides corrugated board being used in packages, it is used as cushions, separators and dividers. These uses also have some standards of their own. With such advances in technology and environmental legislation placing new demands on packaging, there are great opportunities to improve packaging and packaging use, thus adding value to the product.

When the environmental demands on packaging increased in the 1990s, the corrugated board industry became very involved in life cycle assessments (LCA). The industry made data banks available for these assessments and participated in several evaluations. The major advantage for the corrugated board package in comparison with other packaging materials that the industry presented was that the material/package did not need to be returned empty, as the recycling system was well developed and more than 60 per cent of the corrugated board was recycled at the European level. This meant that the evaluation of a distribution system using corrugated board packages looked different from that of other packaging alternatives. The industry attitude was that this packaging difference was significant. Few considerations besides the packaging aspects were considered. In addition, the industry has a recycling system built for the whole European market. This means that the corrugated board packages are collapsed and collected after use and returned to the paper mills in order to be dissolved and remade into new paper material, which will be made into new corrugated board packages. The paper industry has in this way a full system meeting the requirements of legislators.

The plastics industry over the years has focused on production capacity, productivity, efficiency and profitability within its own operations. Its main challenge has been to market and sell commodity products in order to keep the injection moulding machinery running at full speed throughout the year. But for the plastics industry there is a crossroads ahead, concerning the formulating of future business strategies. Who will be the winner in the consolidation race? Which way will the remaining large manufacturers choose: in-house focus on production capacity and a narrow, specialized product range based on a volume-based output focus, or a customer focus, listening and learning more about customer needs in the handling throughout the supply chains, where packaging manufacturers can form partnerships with transport and logistics companies and offer turn-key handling and distribution solutions to their customers?

There are new business developments for the plastic tray industry, such as becoming a facilitator for the food sector. Providing services to complement its product offers has not been explored as a business opportunity. Alternatively, the services have indeed been identified, but turned down for a number of reasons: lack of knowledge on, for example, how to run pool tray systems or how to create financial solutions, not being bold enough to sell the concept to food sector top management levels, etc can be identified as major obstacles. Instead, the plastics industry has in some cases formed alliances with pool companies, such as CHEP, which in turn has approached the food sector with attractive service offers for reusable trays, crates, dollies and pallets (as shown in Figure 4.4).

At the same time as plastic trays were introduced, one-way transport packaging based on cardboard also showed an impressive growth. The most commonly used transport packaging material for fresh food is corrugated (63 per cent). Clearly, there is a market for both types of concepts, but the underlying rationale for the business decisions is important and will be discussed further on in this book. Each packaging material has its advantages and disadvantages that must be considered when stakeholders make new decisions and aim for further efficiency and safety throughout the supply chain.

RETAIL LOGISTICS PACKAGING

Logistics is now a major influence on manufacturers and retailers in their decisions about packaging design. The relationship between key suppliers and key customers in the supply chain is targeted at controlling as much of the supply chain as possible. With many products being commodities, the commercial driver is to create competitive advantage through superior logistics services in order to become or even remain a supplier to the customer. These direct impacts on distribution channels and logistics can be considered through an examination of the costs of packaging. As Table 4.3 shows, there are inherent costs in packaging at various levels and also costs that are created by the handling of the product in the channel. Where these costs can be minimized, there may be advantages to organizations and channels. Table 4.4 looks at some of the trade-offs amongst packaging and other logistics activities. From the point of view of this book, the interesting aspect is the reinforcement of the potential for standardization in packaging and handling.

There is an addition that needs to be made to this list. This is the increasing pace and speed of movement of products along the supply chain as the system changes from a storage method to a rapid replenishment method. This increases the requirement for continuous handling and mixing of products as they move along from producer to retailer. A particular overall issue within efficient unit loads is *interstackability*. It should be possible for all types of trays, crates and boxes to mix on top of each other on a standard pallet, in a roll cage or on a dolly, without the risk of damaging the products, whilst broadly monitoring the shape of the load. Interstackability requirements include

Table 4.3 Elements of packaging costs

Type of Cost	Elements
Development costs	Identification of packaging criteria. Concept search. Design. Models. Sample tooling and samples. Evaluation of samples. Costing and specification writing. Tooling and materials for test marketing. Evaluation of the test market package. Final specification and purchase. Tooling and production. Setting up a quality control system. Start-up.
One-time costs	All development costs above, but mainly 'tooling for production'.
Materials costs	Cost of primary packaging. Special packaging for incoming supplies. Transport for packaging supplies. Storage and handling costs. Loss of packaging materials due to damage, pilferage and over-ordering. Costs of inspection.
Packaging machinery and process costs	Purchase, rental or lease. Service and maintenance. Write-off per unit pack. Power and other services.
Packaging process costs	Direct labour. Indirect labour. Overheads. Incidental materials.
Distribution costs	Storage and warehousing of finished product. Transport to customers. Customer installations. Damage: – direct (cost of replacement); – indirect (loss of sales).

Source: Paine (1990) in Saghir (2004)

Table 4.4 Packaging cost trade-offs with logistics activities

Logistics Activity	Trade-offs
Transportation:	
Increased package information	Decreases shipment delays; increased package information decreases tracking of lost shipments.
Increased package protection	Decreases damage and theft in transit, but increases package weight and transport costs.
Increased standardization	Decreases handling costs, vehicle waiting time for loading and unloading; increased standardization; increases modal choices for shipper and decreases need for specialized transport equipment.
Inventory:	
Increased product protection	Decreased theft, damage, insurance; increases product availability (sales); increases product value and carrying costs.
Warehousing:	
Increased package information	Decreases order filling time, labour cost.
Increased product protection	Increases cube utilization (stacking), but decreases cube utilization by increasing the size of the product dimensions.
Increased standardization	Decreases material handling equipment costs.
Communications:	
Increased package information	Decreases other communications about the product such as telephone calls to track down lost shipments.

Source: Saghir (2002)

demands on how to secure different types of packaging to ensure safe transport and handling conditions. This is an important requirement from a workplace safety perspective, both in distribution centres and on the shop floor, when received deliveries are unpacked and put on shelves. The issues that concern us here are situated in the field of packaging logistics. This binds together the aspects of production, logistics, marketing and environmental concerns and attempts to find solutions that facilitate efficiency and effectiveness in the channel. The logistic aspects that must be taken into consideration are the protection both of the product and of the environment, and the facilitation of transport, handling and storage, as well as how the package provides information about both condition and location of products from production to consumption.

Of particular interest here is the position within retail stores. Particular issues about productivity of handling systems emerge. Several studies have concluded that the high handling costs occur in the store, when unpacking, putting products on the shelves and setting up product displays. There is a large amount of store labour used to put every single case and every single product on to the shelf and to remove packaging. When a supplier is merchandising in a store, this cost is not directly on the store's wage bill. The manufacturer is paying for the staff who work on displaying the products. But when this job is done by the retail staff, it becomes a part of the store's wage budget. Then the retailer is highly motivated to reduce the amount of cost in-store. How much does it cost to handle empty packaging? How much does it cost when retail staff have to spend 15 seconds extra on each box in efforts to open it? How much is spent on collapsing corrugated packaging for recycling?

At a seminar held in Lund, Sweden, in April 2002, participants from manufacturers and retailers concluded that 'if 10 öre are saved in the depot, that is worth 1 krona of saving in the store'. Another conclusion was: 'if you can save one second per packaging in the shop handling, this means annual savings of SEK 12 million [£0.8 million/1 million euros] for one of the three big retailers in Sweden'. This has shifted the packaging design focus on to the impact on productivity at retail. This growing influence of retail logistics on packaging design has given rise to the importance of packaging logistics that takes into consideration all the three dimensions of the manufacturer, logistics and retail.

FRESH FOODS APPLICATIONS

The basic functions of packaging pull in different ways at different times, but the need in fresh food packaging logistics is to design solutions to take care of these tensions as much as possible. The packaging needed to supply fresh food and other types of chilled and frozen products has undergone changes with the development of the retail offer. As packaging is 'a means of ensuring the safe and efficient delivery of goods in sound condition to the ultimate consumer, followed by an efficient reuse and recovery of the packaging combined with an effort maximizing consumer value, sales and hence profit' (Bjärnemo, Jönson and Johnsson, 2000; Paine and Paine, 1983; Saghir,

2004), it is obvious that packaging is crucial for success or failure in the distribution of food. It is also important to recognize that packaging makes up the interface between the product and the environment in which the packaged product will be distributed. Resources invested in production and distribution are wasted if a product is lost through damage or contamination.

Fresh food includes fruit and vegetables, meat, and poultry and fish, as well as dairy products. Normally fruit and vegetables are packed directly into transport packaging, while the other products must be packed in consumer packaging before they are put into transport packaging. Protection of a product is usually ranked as the most important packaging function, as it is the package that will ensure that the product reaches the consumer in the agreed and expected quality. Hence the fragility of a product must be understood, with all the factors that can influence the product during production, transport, handling and storage (Table 4.5). The choice of a suitable packaging system is dependent on what packaging systems are available and the costs and market demand, together with the demands on the product during its life, how far it is transported and stored, the conditions under which the product is handled (ie frozen, chilled, ambient, etc) and climate (temperature, humidity, atmospherc), the microbiology of the product, etc. Some of these issues have been raised in earlier chapters.

A number of further concerns also need to be considered. Washing and cleaning are very important hygiene requirements in food production. The specification of fresh food packaging must include requirements on how the packages should be handled; when reusable plastic trays are used, this is especially important. Hygiene is important in storage areas, store shelves and display areas, as well as in vehicles.

Table 4.5 Factors influencing products during production, transport, handling and storage

External Factors	Protective Packaging Functions
Mechanical Shocks, Vibrations and Compressive Loads	Shock and vibration absorption, compressive strength.
Biological Factors	Resistance.
Gases (O, N, CO_2)	Permeability.
Light	Transmission.
Temperatures	Thermal conductivity.
Water	Resistance and absorption.

All such areas must be cleaned on a regular basis. In Sweden this is a legal requirement, accomplished by the operators within their self-assessment hygienic control programmes, where all activities must be logged and documented in order to be presented to the health authorities at any time. It is important to include hygiene aspects such as conditions at harvesting and packing, the storage of empty packages, the package conditions at packing, and how they are fed into the packaging operation. These hygiene aspects are also important in the retail store, especially how the products are handled when they are put on shelves or other displays, how the products are handled during the emptying of the packages, and how the packaging is removed.

The fresh food chain presents huge challenges for packaging, and there are other influences. One example is the possibility of tracking products all the way from source to final use. In the case of fresh food it is possible to follow every step of the distribution system to ensure that the chill chain – often necessary to keep product freshness – is intact. Any temperature outside a certain tolerance range will influence shelf-life and the quality of the product. The development of e-commerce is another example of new technology that changes the demands on packaging.

CONCLUSIONS

This chapter has been directly concerned with issues of packaging. It has covered briefly some of the issues that are particular to fresh food. The chapter points to changing demands and purposes of packaging. For a long time, packaging was considered mainly from a functional stand-alone viewpoint. Realization has emerged, however, that, by thinking of packaging in a broad sense and from a logistics perspective, new awareness develops. The relationships discussed in this chapter and the breadth of the implications of adopting a packaging logistics approach are summarized in Figure 4.5. One avenue that has opened up has been the role of plastic reusable crates in the food supply chain, at the expense of corrugated and other transport packaging. The pressures for such an approach come from many quarters, including technological change, consumer and retailer demand profiles, handling developments, and governmental and environmental concerns. The consequence of this has been a considerable change in certain supply chains and huge opportunities to develop new approaches.

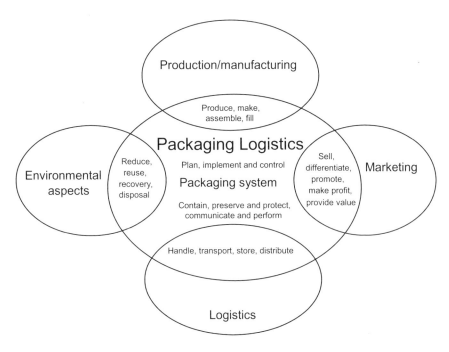

Source: Saghir (2004, p. 61)

Figure 4.5   *Packaging logistics relationships*

Such developments are not without problems, however. The existing providers of corrugated packaging will not let their market share decline without a struggle. Indeed, they would argue that some of the research evidence over environmental impact and hygiene is highly unclear. However, they have also recognized that steps need to be taken to introduce further integration and standardization and to reduce costs and improve efficiency and effectiveness in the supply chain. This more overt packaging logistics approach is emerging strongly. The question, however, is how to achieve internal (company) and external (supply chain) change when there are many different players and many different possibilities. It is to this that we turn in the next chapter.

5 Packaging Logistics Decision Matrix: Change Management

Thus far, the book has considered a number of areas of concern in a sequential fashion. In turn, aspects of change involving retailing, logistics and then packaging have been presented and analysed. Whilst some opportunities to make links across the chapters and topics have been highlighted, in the main the approach has been separate and sequential. However, it should have become obvious that there are considerable interactions amongst these topics and, indeed, it is the overlap amongst them that provides the exciting business opportunities. These interdependencies should be clear. Retail change has an impact on logistics requirements. Packaging to meet new consumer demands needs to be developed. Such new packaging in fresh food needs careful design and handling, both to be effective in the channel and to be attractive to the consumer. Nowhere are such developments more embraced and of interest than in the retail and the fresh food areas. The term 'packaging logistics' has been used to emphasize these interdependencies.

This chapter is thus somewhat different to those that have gone before. Its aim is to integrate the elements from the previous three chapters and to consider how change in packaging logistics channels is best brought about and subsequently managed. It therefore acts as a link between the previous analysis of change and the case studies of change implementation in the next two chapters. Essentially therefore the chapter is in three parts. First, a brief recap on the change components of retailing, logistics and packaging is provided. This focuses on the outer parts of the circles in Figure 5.1. Secondly, the chapter explores in some detail the common areas amongst the topics/circles in the figure, ie the packaging logistics decision matrix. Whilst change is occurring in the areas of retail, packaging and logistics, there are issues about handling these changes. This second part of the chapter therefore considers the organizational issues in companies that are receptive to the change possibilities. This forms the main part of the chapter. Thirdly, the chapter begins to move on to how to implement change, presaging the major cases (Chapter 6) and the more focused application cases (Chapter 7) used in this book.

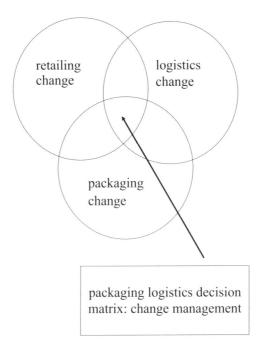

Figure 5.1 *Packaging logistics, retailing and change management*

RETAILING, LOGISTICS AND PACKAGING CHANGE

Chapters 2, 3 and 4 have considered separately aspects of change arising from retailing, logistics and packaging. The main change drivers are summarized in Table 5.1. This summary listing of the aspects of separate change raises a number of issues for packaging logistics decisions:

- Some of these changes are in conflict with other changes and pull companies in separate directions.

- Some changes are driven by concerns about efficiency and effectiveness, whereas others may be more concerned with customer service. Different motivations may lead to conflict or to solutions that point in different directions.

- External change has the potential to influence strongly the extent of change, eg consumer demand patterns and environmental concerns/legislation may override all other changes.

- Given the nature of supply chains, companies may find themselves in varying positions of power and influence and there could be tensions between companies based on their own desires as opposed to channel solutions.

Table 5.1   Change drivers in retailing, logistics and packaging

Retailing	Consumer demographics and demands.
	Consumer lifestyles/incomes and demands.
	Perceptions of time/money.
	Scale and power of retailers.
	Reconstruction of retail formats and functions.
	Globalization of products, sources and retailers.
Logistics	Pressures on costs and services.
	Requirement for efficiency and effectiveness.
	Role of information and technology.
	New management approaches.
	Supply chain orientation.
	Environmental concerns.
Packaging	Technological and materials developments and processes.
	Weight/size balances.
	Cost and service issues.
	Convenience products.
	Safety and protection issues.
	Environmental concerns.

- The sheer volume and breadth of change provide for a considerable variety of potential outcomes. This breadth of potential choices is overwhelming from the point of view both of knowledge acquisition and of implementation.

These complexities mean that, whilst the overlapping area of Figure 5.1 may be quite small visually, the choice sets within the area are considerable. Navigating the packaging logistics decision matrix is quite complex. Doing this and implementing organizational (and possibly channel) change, which is what is implied by the solutions, is a fundamentally difficult task (Twede, 1992). To put this in the form of a question: how do fresh food organizations (retailers, suppliers, producers, etc) manage change concerning packaging logistics? How *could* they organize and manage change, provided they had more in-depth knowledge of change processes concerning packaging logistics and packaging development? What would be the implications for the organizations of such changes? This chapter focuses therefore on those companies working on re-engineering – or even reinventing – their logistics and their packaging solutions. They must be aware that there are *multiple choices* to consider before deciding on new concepts. Furthermore, it is not enough to make a decision – it must be carefully planned, accepted and successfully implemented in order to achieve the desired channel and organizational results.

Obviously adding to the complexity and difficulty is that, within a food supply chain, it is not enough to have a successful change process going on within just one or a few of the companies involved in the supply chain. The change process, to be really effective, must involve *all* actors along the supply chain in order to achieve the full effect and expected/maximized profitability. The drivers and enablers of change have been considered earlier. Here, we also focus on some of the barriers for change in order to explain why companies cannot accomplish the improvements they strive for. By examining barriers to change, and in particular dimensions of organizational change capabilities, it is hoped that some of the barriers within organizations can be overcome. This should provide insights on how to identify the catalysts that may show the way to a more efficient and cost-effective distribution of fresh foods. There are, of course, operational situations where planned changes after implementation provided unexpected and undesired results. Things didn't work. On the other hand, it is obvious that other planned changes have resulted in surprise successes, unexpected but positive spin-offs, providing better business – but no one had planned for such spin-offs. By understanding situations better and by focusing on channel organizational change, perhaps such 'happy accidents' can be more readily foreseen and anticipated and also encouraged.

MANAGING ORGANIZATION CHANGE IN THE SUPPLY CHAIN

Decision making within a food supply chain is a complex process, where there often are several options to consider and many issues to negotiate. Change occurs not only for a single company but also for other supply chain actors. Because of this difference between company and channel perspectives, the work of Kanter (1984) is used here. She explains the drivers and barriers for change, and also points to the significant basic aspects on how to plan and implement change processes. Kanter concludes that there are two types of organizational attitudes or company cultures forming the prerequisites for change processes: the integrative attitude and the segmentalist attitude. This is clearly adaptable to both a company and a supply chain perspective.

The integrative company is a company where employees have access to many types of useful information, collected from both internal and external sources. There is open communication and collaboration between departments, where decentralized decision making results in team building, entrepreneurial spirit, less control and more focus on visions for the future. Problems are treated from a holistic perspective, where attention is given to consequence analyses of different problem-solving actions. Top management encourages innovation and gives support to many change processes. Integrative companies are more proactive than segmentalist companies. An integrative organization shows an openness towards the surrounding society, thereby being able to catch early signals of change in the market. Employees are expected to report to the management on early signs of change in the market.

The segmentalist company is more hierarchical, conservative and traditional. Decisions are made only by the few managers at the highest level. A fear of change is prevalent and problems are dealt with in a manner that focuses on details rather than trying to get the fuller picture. 'Walls' between departments restrict communication and there is little cross-functional team working. Innovation is, as Kanter describes it, 'something given to the R&D department to take care of so no one else has to worry about it'. Control systems allow management to keep a detailed check on the company's past and present operations but this information is not shared with the workforce. Segmentalist companies with a stable market share, well-running operations and a high profitability are the least likely to support new ideas. Employees who try to point at emerging threats are considered disloyal. This type of segmentalist company is the most vulnerable in terms of its inability to manage a rapidly emerging major change in its market.

It is suggested that change processes are more likely to be successful in integrative organizations than in segmentalist ones. But when applying a supply chain perspective, the picture gets more complicated. How can change processes be managed when a supply chain consists of several actors, and where both types of organizations are represented?

The company that strives to drive a change process throughout a supply chain must therefore begin with an analysis of the actors who will be affected by such a change process. Are they ready for change? How do they deal with new demands being put on them? The basic approaches of the component companies are clearly important. Kanter (1984) points to three basic requirements for successful change management: first, the availability of information; second, enough resources provided for the change project; and third, support from top management, in terms of not only economic resources but also commitment to the vision and objectives of the change project. This can be readily understood in terms of an individual business, but across a supply chain it is more difficult.

It is more difficult because a variety of organizations is involved. We therefore want to point at a fourth basic requirement. Before succeeding in getting support, much effort must be put into *gaining acceptance* for the new visions and ideas (from both top management *and* the grass-roots level, and across the supply chain). This, however, immediately raises issues of power in supply chains, as ideas about acceptance are inevitably bound up in questions of power. Who has the power in the supply chain? Is it one single dominant company or an alliance of companies within the supply chain? This aspect is important to take into consideration when performing an analysis of the conditions for starting a change process within a supply chain.

Traditionally, manufacturers have been the drivers and power centres in terms of the packaging and logistics decision making in a food supply chain. However, as has been described in Chapter 2, retailers have successively taken over that power position by using their access to primary consumer information concerning demand, in terms of both quantity and quality (Burt and Sparks, 2003). The large retailers have become channel captains. Channel captaincy is defined here as the member of a marketing channel assuming a leadership role in organizing the system in order to lessen conflict, achieve economies of scale and maximize business impact. Channel captaincy includes logistics skill, packaging skill, handling skill, efficiency focus, environmental/sustainability awareness, etc. In Sweden, the retailers are in the process of taking over the power from the manufacturers and suppliers, whereas in the UK the process is well advanced. As retail internationalization develops, so channel captaincy is exported across the world.

Power has often been utilized in a way that can be described as pure dictatorship. 'Take it or leave it' has been the message from the company that is in the position to decide on logistics and packaging in a supply chain. This ancient way of doing business has been effective for thousands of years, and in many cases it is still effective. The problem is that this produces a chain that is organized for the benefit of one business. Other parallel chains may be organized differently, resulting in overall inefficiency for manufacturers and ultimately for all. It is also the case that such systems tend to use inventory and other 'buffer' techniques to make the service levels work. This again adds cost and/or requires additional efforts.

The emerging awareness of how to build a sustainable supply chain, where every potential for improvement must be explored, is showing another way to use power. The growing importance of active partici-pation *throughout* a supply chain is pushing this development. Large retailers, such as Tesco or IKEA, have learnt the lesson. Instead of just giving orders, 'Do as we say and keep quiet', these large retailers invite their manufacturers and suppliers to establish a dialogue concerning improvements in their supply chain. They are applying a 'learn to like this' attitude towards their suppliers. This is a new type of 'participative dictatorship', where involvement and access to information and new knowledge are basic parameters. Power is being applied, but in a way that works for the good of the sector rather than just the individual company/chain.

This new type of change management based on participative dicta-torships includes learning processes to a large extent. Instead of forcing new methods, new packaging systems or distribution concepts upon the suppliers, these retailers want to show the opportunities that arise with the new aspects. They want to point at innovations that in turn may even lead to improvement upstream, resulting in better business for the manufacturers and suppliers as well. The overall objective is to reach win–win situations through increased collaboration, where both supplier and customer will gain from the new way of working. The associative or collaborative method of working is not new (Dawson and Shaw, 1990), but the method and scope of application into the packaging logistics field marks an extension of the approach.

In terms of decision making, it is important to consider the other extreme to dictatorship: democratic, consensus- or majority-based decision making. This was the type of process method utilized in most parts of the development process in Sweden, when the business-wide, open pool system for returnable transport trays and pallets was designed. This was a time-consuming process. It started in 1992, resulting in a pool system coming into operation in 2000. This case will be considered in detail in the next chapter. A similar product development process driven by Tesco took only two years and is also considered in the next chapter. Tesco was just one, but a very large, powerful organization that was able to influence the extent and pace of change. By contrast, the Swedish decision group included logisticians representing all retailers, all manufacturers, suppliers and growers. The full dimension and lessons of these contrasting cases will be presented in Chapter 6.

The discussion above has so far contrasted integrative with segmentalist companies and suggested that such tendencies affect the propensity and ability to change. This operates at both the company and the supply chain level, though of course the key interest is in the problems brought on by segmentalist companies trying to operate an integrative supply chain. Questions of power and relationships therefore arise, and a further contrast has been drawn between 'dominant designer' supply system change and 'consensus multi-party' approaches. This contrast is explored in more detail in the next chapter. In either case, however, there are some hidden barriers and enablers to change.

Somewhere behind the scenes there are lots of skilled people on many levels in the hierarchies who have the insight, experience, knowledge and understanding of the need for change in products, packaging, logistics, organization, etc. They form an essential starting point when performing the first efforts in the process of gaining acceptance. In some situations these *enablers* have actually already initiated the change process by starting a discussion or pointing at possible ways to solve a problem. They form the prehistory of a change process. Many of the enablers could very well be drivers of change themselves, but for some reason they have decided to position themselves as the silent majority –

in spite of the fact that some of them accomplish results that definitively show the need to persuade them to embrace widespread change.

The *drivers* of change are entrepreneurs who have the ability to see around the obstacles and understand the full picture, and who are able to grasp 'the whole' without losing the detail. The drivers are good communicators, as well as good listeners, and they have the capability of sharing their early vision with others. They are good at establishing relations with the enablers for change, making use of their experience, knowledge and good advice. The drivers are also good at identifying and handling tension, and they know how to fight against the barriers to change.

Obviously there is a wide range of *barriers* and obstacles, more than enough to chill the most enthusiastic drivers, enablers and entrepreneurial spirit. Opposition and resistance can be active or passive. There are also two different time-frames for opposition. Early opposition can be seen as scepticism, as well as reluctance to commit time and resources. People showing an early opposition may say that they have other obligations that are more important, or they conclude that 'we tried to do that five [or 10 or 15] years ago, and it did not work'. Later opposition can emerge quickly, surprising the drivers of change. Some people start to challenge specific details of the plan that is unfolding. At a late stage they suddenly realize that the change will affect them personally in a negative way or will affect their close environment.

Active opposition may be easier to handle. It is often possible to discuss with people who tell you that they are against proposed action. The verbal argumentation is easier to handle than silent opposition. When dealing with passive opposition and resistance, certain common types can be identified. Some people are critics concerning specific details of the plan – many of them lack the ability to grasp the full picture. Not responding to requests is another typical form of passive opposition. Not being available is another way of protesting. Others show their unavailability by preferring to work with other projects. These common types of passive opposition can be identified where office work takes place. At the grass-roots level, these types of opposition may occur, but here another type of passive opposition is more likely to be encountered. In warehouses and distribution centres, problems with passivity or 'foot dragging' are more common – even if 'foot dragging' may occur in offices as well.

One important aspect concerning 'foot dragging' must be highlighted. Passivity of any kind is in many ways more efficient than open, verbal opposition. It is the only 'weapon' that the most powerless people can use. Furthermore, it is a comfortable weapon, since the opponents using it don't have to put themselves in tricky situations where they have to say no and provide their arguments for it. Finally, foot dragging is a way to buy time and delay something happening that will disturb the normal, everyday working routines.

When the impending change is about to happen in real life, many critics who have kept quiet during the planning processes become actively resistant. One possible reason for this is that latent discontent with other issues may become mobilized, as the change process can work as a catalyst, exposing previously hidden problems.

When a driver of change encounters all or some of the active and passive resistance, there are some ways to deal with it by disarming the opponents. At first, the method of waiting it out can be applied, showing patience with the opponents and trying to wear them down with fact-based argumentation. Appealing to larger principles may be one way of argumentation. In some cases it may be enough to say that 'this has been decided by top management'. Inviting the opponent in, offering interesting tasks to be undertaken, is another way of dealing with individual opponents. It is better to have certain people with you than against you, but in such cases it is important that the process is transparent and open, and aligns people, processes and technology (West and Sparks, 2004).

PACKAGING LOGISTICS DECISION MATRIX: CHANGE MANAGEMENT

The concepts above can now be applied to the food supply chain system by considering change management processes in the packaging logistics decision matrix, in particular how the concepts of segmentalist and integrative approaches are adopted at the company and supply chain levels, and pathways to implement change are considered.

It is suggested in Figure 5.2 that integrative companies in integrative supply chains (sector D) are more likely to succeed with their change processes than the other combinations. Unfortunately, this ideal situation is seldom seen in a food supply chain – or in any other supply chain formed by a number of companies, possibly because of traditional approaches to supply chain development and the accretion of historical processes. How therefore can an integrative company in a segmentalist-influenced supply chain solve the problem of managing change within segmentalist companies? What role has the integrative

Abilities and attitudes:

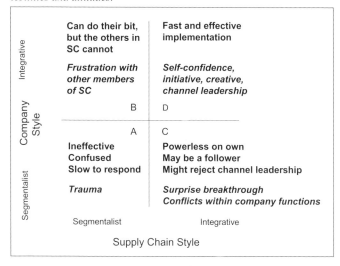

Organizational styles:

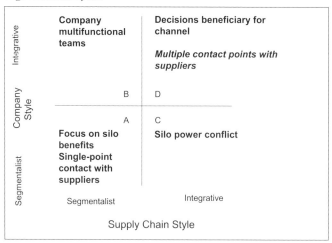

Figure 5.2   *Integrative and segmentalist supply chains and companies*

company that has the vision of improving customer value, product value or system value? If it is a large retailer, the chance of achieving success is better than if it is a small supplier. The large retailer can use its power as the customer for the other actors in the supply chain. The situation, however, is not hopeless for the small supplier that is integrative and innovative and has visions for change. Being innovative, this company may identify other companies within the supply chain that also can be defined as integrative and innovative. While forming an alliance, they will gain power and increase the capacity to gain acceptance from the slow, non-visionary segmentalist companies.

In Figure 5.3, in the case of Route A, the company with a segmentalist company style decides to switch to the integrative attitude. The company has to overcome its silo conflicts and generate multifunctional teams to address its supply chain issues. This results in an improvement of the company's position, enabling it to leverage any collaboration that is developing between elements of the supply chain network. The leadership model to be applied is to make the company act as a nodal point, encouraging cooperation within the supply chain. In some instances the company can develop as the channel captain if it holds the balance of power and influence within the channel.

The channel captain model can be taken by a company that not only takes Route A but acts as a catalyst for the supply chain to be transformed from segmentalist to an integrative cooperative whole. The company is creative and identifies the channel benefits early in the competitive process. It repositions both itself and the elements of the supply chain network to realize and gain the channel cooperation benefits.

In Figure 5.3, a company with a segmentalist company style has a choice: it can either stagnate or it can develop. If it continues in its own silo conflict, power imbalance and power struggle, while the other elements in the supply chain are collaborating to gain channel benefits, or if the company applies the *blocker model*, the company will stagnate and isolate itself from the other elements of the supply chain. It can be identified as a blocker by the others, which can then deselect it so that it is excluded from the supply chain and from access to the marketplace. On the other hand, if the *follower model* is applied by the company, which develops and sees the strategic change that is going on in the supply chain and the competitive marketplace, and if it can overcome its internal silo conflicts, it can gain long-term competitive advantage from the channel benefits (Route B).

This transformation of supply chains is vitally important not only for the companies and supply chains involved but also as examples of what may be possible in other situations. A number of brief illustrations make the point:

- The example of Zara's supply chain in fashion is held up as a modern supply chain that has provided the company with competitive advantage (brief details can be found in Sparks, 2004). This was developed both internally and by external associations with forward-thinking partners. One consequence,

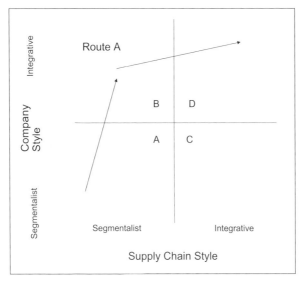

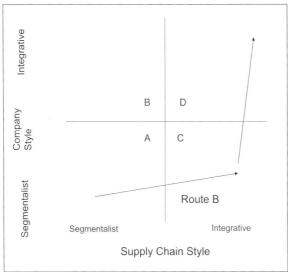

Figure 5.3   *Routeways to change in supply chains*

however, has been to make other clothing and fashion retailers consider their own supply chain activities in an attempt to match Zara. Change becomes an externally driven imperative.

- The convenience store sector in Japan is a retail phenomenon and, within that, Seven-Eleven Japan is utterly remarkable. As Sparks

(1995, 2000a) shows, Seven-Eleven Japan chose not to develop its supply chains along traditional Japanese lines but rather took the opportunity to build new patterns, processes, systems and partners. Through its incredible performance record over 30 years, Seven-Eleven Japan has forced competitors to rethink their supply systems.

- As Tesco have internationalized, so they have taken their model distribution operation (Smith and Sparks, 2004) abroad. This has involved effective reconfiguration of supply systems in a variety of countries and included changes to patterns of work, supply and business relationships. Tesco efficiency and power have provided a benchmark in countries such as Poland and Thailand. Interestingly, Wal-Mart in Germany, in a much less powerful position, and with concerted opposition, has failed thus far in its ability to transform German food retail logistics.

- Coles Myer, the Australian retailer, has over the last few years been overhauling its supply systems. The aim has been to produce substantial cost savings. The CEO has been reported as describing this as 'a major paradigm shift'. However, whilst the overhaul is of such significance for the company and possibly for Australian retailing, the CEO did go on to comment that 'the planned supply overhaul is no different to what has already occurred in Europe and North America. We are arguably a decade behind the northern hemisphere. This is not pioneering, this is not going off and doing things that haven't been tried or done somewhere else in the world' (*M&M Planet Retail*, 25 September 2003).

These examples have not always worked smoothly from the start. They represent the current position in a long, ongoing process of change that is affecting all major supply chains in retailing across the world.

THE IMPLEMENTATION STAGE

Businesses of course confront hurdles and opportunities, which have to be managed properly. In many cases, a full roll-out on a large scale is very risky in terms of cost and risk of losing confidence. Pilot successes are one of the most powerful tools when implementing full-scale roll-outs. Pilot projects provide valuable data and experience to make use of further on. The human factors are of great value here: after the achievement of one or a few successful pilot schemes, there are a number of people who have learnt something new. Their participation in the full-scale roll-out is most valuable, as they can work as teachers, mentors or supporters. Their positive attitude must be used to encourage others who still haven't decided that they approve of the upcoming change. Pilot projects also provide useful information on the need for adjustments in the planning of the full-scale implementation. In some cases the pilots indicate that there is a need for a total rescheduling of the full-scale implementation.

When performing the full-scale implementation of a new method, new packaging system, new distribution model, etc, it cannot be emphasized strongly enough how important it is to communicate with all the people involved. The closer and more personal the communication, the better. Quick feedback on early results is vital to morale and 'fighting spirit' in the change process. It is even important to communicate negative results, in order to encourage people to come up with solutions on how to handle the upcoming problems.

The value of top management involvement during the first critical days must also be underlined. The physical presence of a CEO or a logistics and procurement director brings the message of the importance of achieving success. In an integrative company, people are quite used to seeing their top managers on the shop floor, but their presence is still valuable since it shows their commitment to the process.

No matter how well planned a change process is, there will always be unexpected results. If they are positive, they are welcomed as an added value to the results. But if unexpected results are negative, demonstrating large problems in the implementation, there is an immediate need for analysis, which must result in fast decision making on how to eliminate or minimize the negative effects. Access to all relevant information is of course an important factor when performing an analysis of the unexpected results. It is also highly valuable to have access to and availability of open communication with all parties involved in order to be provided with reliable information.

In some cases, especially in segmentalist companies involved in segmentalist supply chains, unexpected results may result in a trauma that paralyses all types of change processes for a long time. However, there may be another possible reaction, which in turn may show the way for a segmentalist company to become integrative. As described above, large segmentalist companies that have been market leaders for a long time are not aware enough to listen to early warning signals concerning changes in the marketplace. In that case, a change process failure resulting in a traumatic situation may be the trigger point to start the company waking up from the 'fat cat syndrome' in order to revitalize its ability to follow developments in the market. An analogy might be that many alcoholics must fall to the deepest level of humiliation before they are responsive and ready to receive treatment. A recent retail example (2004/05) might be the major trauma suffered by Sainsbury as they attempted to stop their decline from number 1 in the UK. A huge investment in distribution facilities and systems proved incapable of delivering products properly to stores and has been ridiculed in the trade press. Perhaps the need for radical change *throughout* the business follows from this damaging failure to get products on to the shop shelves. Indeed, their most recent more radical and integrated business changes do seem to be re-energizing the business and bringing positive results.

SUMMARY

This chapter has been concerned with the concepts of change management in the packaging logistics decision matrix. It points to the need for a full consideration of company and supply chain positions in order to implement successful change. Issues of power and channel captaincy have been confronted with more consensual possibilities. The discussion has, however, been somewhat abstract and so it is to concrete examples that we now turn. The next chapter looks at the contrasting approaches in two major cases from the UK and Sweden. This is then supplemented in Chapter 7 by a number of smaller, focused application cases. Lessons from all of these in the light of the discussion in this chapter are then drawn in Chapter 8.

6

Major Case Studies

This chapter presents two major case studies of change in the packaging logistics supply chain. The intention is to use these two different approaches, one from the UK and one from Sweden, to contrast the possibilities in organizing packaging logistics and managing change in the supply chain. One of the purposes of this chapter is to help businesses understand the situations that may confront them and the opportunities available. The two case studies are presented in turn and then some lessons and conclusions are drawn. The first study is about the implementation of the second-generation tray in Tesco's supply chain in the UK. The second case is on the development of a multiparty nationwide pool in Sweden.

IMPLEMENTING THE SECOND-GENERATION TRAY IN TESCO'S SUPPLY CHAIN

Tesco is one of the leading food retailers in the world (see Seth and Randall, 2005). It has become the number one food retailer in the UK (Burt and Sparks, 2003) and now has stores across Eastern Europe and

Asia. As a leading retailer, it has been subjected to considerable investigation by researchers and analysts. Within this, the transformation of Tesco's distribution has been particularly studied, and it is within this context that the case study is developed. Readers wanting further information on the Tesco distribution systems should refer to the earlier work of Smith and Sparks (Smith, 1998; Smith and Sparks, 1993, 2004; Sparks, 1986) and the references in those readings.

The case study presented here has been developed and researched in two ways. One of the authors (David Smith) was involved in the implementation of the system and so is a participant researcher. Subsequent to the case he has been engaged in research and consultancy on logistics broadly for various clients and has thus also developed a more reflective view of the activities in which he was once engaged.

The Tesco case study is an example of the rapid implementation of a national strategy for recycling packaging. The impending EU legislation in the early 1990s on packaging recycling schemes, with its financial penalties, forced retailers and suppliers to conduct a strategic review of their practices for disposing of secondary packaging at the retail store. The existing system saw secondary packaging either thrown away or recycled in a cumbersome way. Tesco, as a leading food retailer, decided to act quickly to get ahead of the legislation and implement a radically new approach for its stores and suppliers.

The context for this development within the Tesco supply chain has several aspects that are worth documenting before getting into the detail of the case study. Within the store product range, there had been strong growth in the chilled fresh food categories. The logistics and supply chain processes had speeded up to provide customers with fresher product that lasted longer in the home. This focus on the rapid handling of fresh foods from supplier to retail shelf resulted in much less stock being held in the supply chain, as time spent standing still was time taken from the shelf-life available to the consumer. At the retail store there was an examination of the labour costs of putting product on shelves, and new methods were devised to help retail staff work more effectively. These trends formed the background for the Tesco development of a second-generation plastic tray and a national network of recycling service units.

The timetable of events was compressed to get ahead of the legislation deadlines, and can be divided into three phases. The first phase, 1990–92, involved the board decision to proceed. The second phase, 1992–94, was the implementation of the national recycling network with the second-generation plastic tray. The third phase, 1995–97, was the continued effort to grow the recycling business using the plastic tray.

The first phase, from 1990 to 1992, involved the board decision to proceed with a new approach for disposing of secondary packaging by the retail stores through the setting up of specialized recycling service units that would recycle the plastic and cardboard and clean the increasing volume of plastic trays so they could be reused by the suppliers. This strategy repositioned the impending EU legislation on recycling from a threat into a business opportunity. The board's decision was based on an assessment of the costs and benefits. There were the costs of change and implementation that were set against the penalties being imposed by the EU legislation. The benefits were to be found throughout the business, retail, commercial, logistics, suppliers and the environment. Retail were able to work more productively in-store using the plastic tray for displaying products, especially fruit and vegetables. The commercial division prioritized which product groups would benefit from lower costs in using the plastic tray rather than corrugated secondary packaging. Logistics improved their handling and stacking using the plastic tray. Suppliers paid less by using the plastic tray. The environmental benefits contributed to the reputation of Tesco as a company acting as a good citizen.

The implementation phase, from 1992 to 1994, was intense and compressed to get ahead of the legislation deadlines. The national network of recycling service units needed to be located next to the composite distribution centres that handled the fresh food product range. All the cardboard and plastic that used to be disposed of locally through the store waste compactors, as well as the plastic trays, was going to be collected from the stores by the composite delivery vehicles on their return journeys. Suppliers would then be able to collect the trays they needed after their deliveries to the distribution centre. It was decided to give the contract for the operation of these recycling service units to one contractor as part of the Tesco strategy to benefit from applying best practice throughout the network. There was a standard design for all the recycling service units. This design needed to balance the capacity and space for the operation in order to keep the costs of the land and building as low as possible. One of the influences on the amount of space required was the empty nesting ratio of the plastic tray. The first-generation tray had a ratio of 2:1. The target for the second-generation tray was 4:1. This was not an easy task at the time, but the tray manufacturer did eventually succeed. The commercial division had the task of prioritizing which product groups should go into plastic trays and then instilling the new disciplines with those suppliers. The implementation beat the legislation deadline, and the first recycling service unit was officially opened by the Minister of Agriculture and the Environment, John Gummer, in 1995. He identified the occasion as an example of good practice and initiative for the UK environmental agenda.

From 1995 to 1997, there was a phase of growing the number of products using plastic trays to reach an annual volume of 100 million. The unit cost of a plastic tray trip was linked to the total volume going through the recycling service unit network. The first product group had been fresh fruit and vegetables, as there was a high cost to the secondary packaging of good-quality corrugated board. The next product group was fresh meat and poultry, which had by that time been reorganized into a centralized factory production system, with the fully prepared meat and poultry going directly into the plastic trays and quickly through the logistics supply chain to the retail store, with no stock being held in the composite distribution centres. The production quantity was determined by the anticipated retail sales, with no buffer stock in the supply chain. The plastic trays fully protected the product during its handling and assembly into store orders in distribution. The next set of product groups were lighter in weight with a lower corrugated cost and needed a lower cost for the use of the plastic tray to be economical. This was now possible, as the volume moved through to a higher level, justifying a reduction. The commercial, retail, supply chain and logistics cost benefits were evaluated to prioritize the selection of the next product group. This was specialist bakery products, such as croissants and pastries. By 2004, Tesco had continued to grow the business in plastic trays to a stock holding of 7.5 million trays and an annual throughput of 200 million movements. Figure 6.1 illustrates the retail use of such trays.

A valuable part of the implementation with the suppliers of these products was a supplier day held at a recycling service unit. A small group of suppliers and representatives from commercial, technical, supply chain, logistics and retail worked together to agree the optimum configuration of products in a tray and discuss the implications of the change. These events were highly successful in gaining the positive involvement of the suppliers in this change process. This had big implications for their production and packaging methods. During this phase there was also a broader assessment of the feedback from the suppliers about the implications for the whole industry servicing the retailers. The outcome of this review was a consensus on a single design that *all the retailers* would use. This eliminated the cost of complication for the suppliers if each retailer had continued to insist on using its own distinct design.

Recycling service unit operation and the second-generation plastic tray

The purpose of a recycling service unit (RSU) is to minimize the volume of secondary packaging that has to go into landfill by recycling and reusing as much as possible. Corrugated board and plastic wrapping are recycled back to industry. The plastic trays are reused many times within the supply chain. At the end of their life they are shredded, forming raw material for manufacturing of new plastic trays or pallets.

The processes that take place at a recycling service unit vary for the different categories of cardboard, plastic wrapping and plastic trays. They are sorted on their arrival from the stores into the different sections for recycling or washing. The plastic wrapping and cardboard are placed into separate compactors that create bales that are then recycled. They are sold into the marketplace as a national contract, which results in better prices than they had before with each store negotiating separately.

Corrugated board secondary packaging in the retail supply chain continues to exist for a considerable proportion of goods. The retail store staff flatten the empty cardboard boxes and return them in roll cages to the RSU. The corrugated board is then compacted into mill-size bales of 600 kilograms, which are sent under contract for recycling to the paper mills. The transport to the paper mill operates on a rotating system. Empty trailers are stationed at the RSU and, as each one is loaded up, it is taken away and another empty trailer left in its place. The volume that Tesco stores generate is about 100,000 tons, which equates to the production volume of a medium-size paper mill. There is a similar process for the plastic wrapping. The empty plastic trays are sorted by size at the retail store and sent back to the RSU for washing and reissuing to suppliers.

The floor area of the recycling service units was a critical part of the design, given their land and build costs in the business case. The final design was 75,000 square feet (c 7,000 square metres) with sections for goods in corrugated baling, plastic baling, tray-washing facilities, clean tray storage and despatch. This was a direct result of the improved empty nesting ratio of 4:1 for the second-generation

Figure 6.1   *The retail use of plastic trays in Tesco* (source: *author photographs, 2004*)

Figure 6.1a

plastic tray. As the first-generation plastic tray nested at half this space efficiency (2:1), its use would have increased the amount of physical space needed for the goods-in area and the storage of the washed trays to a larger RSU footprint of 100,000 square feet. In the business case, the footprint size of the RSU was a critical cost factor that needed to be controlled. This motivated the development of a second-generation tray empty nesting ratio of 4:1 with the same internal cube.

Figure 6.1b

The amount of product in plastic trays is about 15 per cent of the total volume of goods sold. There are four tray washing machines in each RSU, which gives the operation a good capacity even to do work for other companies. The waste water is recycled and technologists check the water and trays for cleanliness to ensure that they come out at the proper level of hygiene for reuse outside the high-care environment of food production. They are then stacked on pallets at standardized heights and quantities so the supplier can always be sure of having the correct number of trays simply by counting the number of pallets collected. The clean trays are stored and issued on a rotating basis to suppliers, who have a 36-hour window agreed with the operation to collect clean trays. The suppliers can choose to collect their clean trays from an RSU local to their manufacturing facility, which would reduce their transport costs and provide more flexibility to keep their stocks of clean trays at the right operating level.

The second-generation plastic tray has a footprint of 600 by 400 millimetres, and there is a half-tray with a footprint of 300 by 400 millimetres. They fit both the Euro pallet and the UK pallet. They have different heights to suit different types of products, which together with a folding and adjustable handle improve the space efficiency. An inefficient use of space was one of the criticisms made of the first-generation plastic tray system compared to the use of corrugated secondary packaging, which is designed to fit closely to its products. There was considerable development effort at the design stage to find workable solutions that would retain the benefits of rapid handling and product protection, which are strong features of the plastic tray system, but with minimal loss of space efficiency. The adjustable bale arm was the chosen design solution, which was made possible with the improvements in plastic materials.

The second-generation 600 by 400 millimetre plastic tray was designed as a modular system that would work efficiently with other equipment in the handling and transport process along the supply chain from supplier to store. Whilst it fits both the Euro and the UK pallet dimensions, a further part of the modular system design development at that time was a dolly. This is a plastic base on wheels that stacks 50 trays in two columns of 25 with a clip at the top designed to hold them in place. The use of dollies provided productivity benefits in retail store handling, warehouse handling and transport cube efficiency. At the retail store and in the warehouse assembly dollies are very popular, as they are easy to move around and, when empty, stack on each other, which uses less space. The transport cube is more efficient, as a standard length 13-metre trailer will hold 60 dollies compared to 45 roll cages. This advantage comes about because the dolly footprint is smaller than that of a roll cage, which has sides to hold the product secure. The equipment cost of a dolly is lower than that of a roll cage. Figure 6.2 shows dollies in retail use in the supply chain.

The design development of this entire second-generation plastic tray and dolly system provided supply chain, logistics and retail productivity and utilization efficiencies. These were an essential part of the transformation from the earlier more static storage to the modern dynamic, fast-moving and tailored volumes of products that resulted in no stock being held in the supply chain, except what was in transit between suppliers, distribution and stores.

Analysis

This case study can be further analysed to reveal some of the underlying forces that made this successful. The discussion begins with the company culture and then more closely examines the challenges of the change agenda, which leads into some broader conclusions.

Figure 6.2   *The retail use of dollies in Tesco* (source: *author photograph, 2005)*

The company culture in Tesco is set by the vision of the board for the company's mission to serve consumers to obtain their lifetime loyalty. This vision drives forward national change within the company. Although it is a large business, it is agile and able to implement rapid change in the organization through its ability to motivate staff and suppliers by sharing its vision and strategic direction. One aspect of serving consumers for their lifetime loyalty is the contribution of the company through its policies as a good citizen within the global community. Although each consumer as an individual has very little power, consumers still have the freedom of choice in their buying power through their purchases, which means that they can influence big companies to get them to care for the environment as good citizens. In the mid-1990s, Tesco was voted the most admired company by business people and achieved the status of being highly trusted by ordinary people, which is a remarkable dimension to corporate retail brand value (Burt and Sparks, 2003). For a food store to be trusted for its values is a profound reflection of how important the store's brand had become to the ordinary consumer. In this case study, a main board director who had the responsibility for the initiative drove the change within the company. This initiative would bring benefits for the consumer and the environment, as well as the retail, logistics and supply chain operations. This together with the increased power and leadership role of the retailer placed Tesco in a strong position to grasp the challenge of the new recycling legislation and turn it into a commercial advantage.

At the time of the case study, Tesco had already implemented key changes to its infrastructure for information technology, and supply chain and temperature controlled logistics (Smith and Sparks, 1993; Sparks, 1986). This placed it in a very good position to develop a national strategy of recycling service units alongside each of its multi-temperature composite distribution centres. These handled the most volatile and sensitive food products, which were the very products that it was logical to transfer into the plastic tray system. This transformation in retail supply was an evolution from storage to rapid handling by all the parties along the chain. Logistics became an approach focused on movement and no longer about holding stock. This faster pace of logistics was a powerful driving force, and some of the conflict and change management during this transition in the supply chain operation arose because the old way of doing logistics for storage did not meet the need for faster handling and the very rapid movement of the goods from the supplier to the retail store. However, suppliers who had earlier experiences of successful change by Tesco were more able to give their credibility to this development in the recycling strategy.

There were several items on the agenda for change in this process of implementing the national recycling strategy and the second-generation plastic tray at retail, logistics and the suppliers. Beginning with the focus on retail, the efficiency of the total supply chain had improved so much that Tesco was giving its attention to the cost of handling and displaying product in the retail store and to finding ways of improving productivity and so reducing cost by working more effectively. At that time it was estimated that 30 to 50 per cent of supply chain cost was in the retail store moving the goods from the delivery vehicle to the shelf for the consumer (the so-called last 50 yards). The retail productivity driver continued to be a powerful force in the organization and had a strong influence on the design of the second-generation plastic tray. This was developed in a very short time span of two years and would later have a much wider impact with far-reaching implications beyond the company's own supply chain. (Figure 6.3 shows the same-size trays in other food retailers in the UK, albeit covered up in Figure 6.3e for merchandising and promotional reasons.)

The internal retail studies had quantified the productivity benefit of the introduction of plastic trays. These reduced the time needed to put stock out on the shelves for consumers and eliminated the effort of removing corrugated packaging from the store. Fresh produce had been the first product group selected to go into plastic trays, as these could be placed directly into the display stands for customers who wanted to handle and select products individually. This was recognized by retail management, who created a good selling environment for this to happen. Such produce was placed close to the entrance of a food store in open trays so that the customers could immediately start into the shopping routine in a way that is personal, selective and tactile.

What, then, are the criteria for packaging in the retail and logistics operations? Retail want packaging that protects the product and is easy to handle, easy to open and easy to recycle. The logistics operation needed packaging that protected the products throughout the supply chain, especially at those points where it is stacked with different products at the supplier and the consolidation centre and at the composite distribution centre where the store orders are assembled. The distribution centre is a good location from which to design packaging, as the consequences of it being stacked with different products can be studied. This aspect of the operation is hidden from the supplier and so is not usually taken into account in the traditional design configuration of corrugated packaging.

It is worth exploring this further. The pace at which a composite logistics operation is working, especially from 6 pm to midnight, is so intense and so fast that management has to design a store order assembly system that is as efficient as possible, because it is at the heart of packaging logistics. The logistics operation is manually intense, and the cost of labour is a high proportion of the annual expenditure budget. Operational management are always seeking better ways to work that are smarter, rather than just making people work harder. It is

Figure 6.3   *Plastic packaging in UK stores*

Figure 6.3a   *Asda* (source: *author photograph, 2002*)

Figure 6.3b   *Southern Co-operative* (source: *reproduced with permission, 2004*)

Figure 6.3c   *Somerfield at Mace* (source: *author photograph*)

Figure 6.3d   *Asda* (source: *author photograph, 2004*)

Figure 6.3e   *Asda* (source: *author photograph, 2004*)

a matter of improving productivity and volume throughput and at the same time ensuring the product is protected properly. When the assemblers are given their store assignments to pick, they are expected to work accurately as well as quickly. It is very important for the operation that the assembler selects the right product for the right store. This is a fundamental discipline, given the fast pace at which they are operating. On many occasions, corrugated packaging did not stand up to the challenge, and it soon became evident that the second-generation plastic tray was the right solution. The challenge for corrugated was too great. This was demonstrated during a visit in 1997 to a composite distribution centre by an international group of cardboard packaging experts, who could see for themselves that the second-generation plastic tray performed well compared to corrugated boxes.

There were important challenges for the suppliers when implementing this recycling strategy with the second-generation plastic tray. Many of these suppliers had already experienced the benefits of successful change by Tesco and were open to the credibility of the new recycling strategy. During the phase of growing the use of the plastic tray business, a multifunctional team from Tesco would invite suppliers in small groups to visit an RSU and ask them to bring along their products. After an induction and walk around the RSU, the suppliers were normally impressed with the physical scale of the operation. However, they had issues to discuss: some could be resolved quickly; others were more difficult. For example, the supplier knew that corrugated boxes provided a good-quality product branding with coloured slogans, designs and even pictures. When a whole display of boxes was put out in the store it provided a very strong impact. Plastic trays did not offer this. But this was an issue they had to weigh up for themselves, and they had to find other ways of promoting their brand image.

The suppliers would try their products in the different sizes of plastic tray and agree with commercial and retail the quantity of units and the size of the tray. There were also some important additional benefits from having a family of tray sizes especially for promotion lines. For example, the shallow tray might be right for their product. But during a promotion campaign they could justify putting two layers of the product and using a deep tray, which would also improve handling and logistics efficiency. Getting a balance between shallow and deep trays from the RSU was easy; they might have 10 lines in total with two on promotion at any one time. If the actual volume varied from the forecast then they did not have a panic about specially printed corrugated packaging if the volume was up or a waste of printed packaging if the volume was down. This application for promotions reduces the total cost of the plastic tray against the corrugated boxes. When companies are making a promotion campaign it is a way of assisting the obtained margin.

Once the suppliers had the opportunity to talk through their issues and agree solutions with the different members of the Tesco team, they were better prepared to return to their own operations and talk through the changes with their production and despatch teams. These visits were a valuable contribution to the success of growing the tray business. There were some special dynamics. If an individual supplier was contacted in isolation, then the conversation would centre on particular issues preventing the implementation of the proposed change. This could be termed a tactical response. However, when the small group were together at the RSU there were the benefits of group dynamics. Some suppliers were very positive when others brought forward their issues. The scale of the physical operation, together with the presence of the multifunctional team from Tesco, created a conviction that this was going to be part of a successful business development. They were faced with a more strategic than tactical choice. Did they want to be part of this future or not? Once they had decided to join in the new strategy they put more effort into finding solutions to overcome any production and despatch issues. This strategic choice was a channel decision. It was a decision to join the direction of the retail leadership. It is an example of Tesco acting as the channel leader or channel captain and organizing the supply chain efficiencies (Burt and Sparks, 2003).

The repercussions of the second-generation tray went much further than the Tesco supply chain. Manufacturers said that they understood the application and benefits of the plastics trays but pointed out that there were different sizes and specifications from the different retailers. This puts demands of complexity into their production and distribution processes. The manufacturers asked the retailers to act together and agree a common standard. This they eventually did.

Summary

This case study is an example of a company that is not only internally integrated but also integrated within its supply chain. Tesco was in a position of strength and became the channel leader. The lessons from this will be discussed later in this chapter and in Chapters 8 and 9.

THE DEVELOPMENT OF A MULTI-PARTY NATIONWIDE POOL SYSTEM IN SWEDEN

This case study is about a multi-party-based development and decision process, which eventually resulted in a nationwide packaging pool system in Sweden (see Svenska Retursystem AB, 2003). Planning and implementing such a pool system is a complex process. This case focuses on the driving forces in the development and decision processes. A fuller version can be found in Gustafsson (2005).

After several years of discussions, tests, investigations and new tests, suppliers and retailers within the Swedish business sector for food and commodities formed a jointly owned non-profit company in 1997, which started its physical operations in 2000. This company, Svenska Retursystem AB (www.retursystem.se), has the mission to introduce returnable transport packaging into the Swedish food supply chains. The product range includes a family of nestable and interstackable plastic trays and plastic pallets in two sizes. This pool system is unique, since it is the only open, business-wide and national pool system in operation in the world. It is also an example of a development where there has been no clearly dominant or driving actor. Instead the process has been driven by suppliers and retailers in a negotiation- and majority-based consensus way of decision making.

During 1992–99, a group of logistics specialists within the Swedish food supply chains took part in a development process, which included much learning and new thinking. The process contained eight separate missions, which are described in Table 6.1. The collection of data is based on interviews by Kerstin Gustafsson (see also Gustafsson, 2005). Documents from meetings support the analyses of the interviews.

Definitions and terminology

This case is concerned with returnable trays, in a packaging pool system. Different types of transport packaging and pool systems can be defined in order of complexity.

At first, the design of the packaging must meet certain requirements. The returnable transport packaging that is designed to fit just one specific type of product is of course quite easy to design, as it is more or less tailor-made. The designer's task gets more complicated when the returnable transport packaging is being planned for multi-product purposes, where the tray (or the family of trays) must be suitable to

Table 6.1 The Swedish missions

Working Group 1:
1. Identification of the potential of the pool concept and securing government support.
2. Large-scale pilot test.
3. Administrative system developments for the pool system (postponed to mission 8).
4. Design of a material-neutral functional standard for half-pallets.
5. Concept design of a pool system for returnable trays for vegetables.

Working Group 2:
6. Specification of the requirements for a business-wide returnable tray (tender process).
7. Environmental evaluation of a plastic tray.
8. Administrative system developments for the pool system and the establishment of a member-owned pool company.

many types of product groups (eg fruit and vegetables, dry groceries, bread, meat and poultry, dairy products and cheese).

The next step is to decide the pool system design. A few different types of pool systems can be identified, serving certain types of packaging logistics requirements, starting from simple, closed single-loop pool systems running from one supplier to one customer and then back to the supplier. The complexity is increasing when starting a multi-loop pool system, which can go from one supplier to many customers and then back to the supplier. Another type of pool system on this level is when one large customer provides a number of suppliers with customer-owned returnable transport packaging (this is common within the automotive industry). The third, and most complicated, level is an *open-loop pool system*, where many suppliers and many customers are members of the pool system. At this level, there is a need to establish rules in order to keep loss of packaging and costs down by using deposits or fees to be paid by those who are using pool packaging. This is similar to the Chep pallet system.

For all the above-mentioned types of returnable packaging systems, there are four main success factors that determine the profitability and usability of the system (Stahre, 1996). The first success factor is to establish rules that enable a high speed of circulation of packaging items, defined as *trips per year*. Another factor, already mentioned above, is to keep the loss ratio of packaging items to a minimum level. Thirdly, the geographical coverage and transport costs must be carefully considered. Finally, the fourth key success parameter is to plan the need for packaging in order to meet seasonal variations (growing seasons as well as holiday seasons). The worst peaks, normally before Christmas, cannot be the denominator for the dimensioning of a pool system. Extreme peaks must be solved by using one-way packaging when returnable packaging is scarce.

Working Group 1, 1992–94

In 1992, this process of setting up a system in Sweden started when the first working group was formed. The members of this group represented a wide spectrum of actors in the Swedish food supply chain: growers, manufacturers, transporters, wholesalers and retailers. The chair was a senior retailing logistics expert, well known and respected for his deep knowledge of the business sector. This group was active during three years, 1992–94. This first group completed five of the eight missions that can be identified as separate parts of the process (see Table 6.1).

Initially in 1992, the most important issue was to make sure that all group members were equally aware of the potential of the pool concept. The overall objective was to create a packaging system with lower supply chain total cost. Additional objectives were increased product quality due to less transport damage, improved ergonomics and less time-consuming in-store handling, as well as waste reduction.

This first mission also included the task of selling the vision to some governmental agencies in order to obtain the necessary financing of the upcoming development process. At an early stage it was concluded by the working group members that government agencies could be suitable project sponsors, as the group thought that a government-sponsored process would have a higher credibility and authorization than if the actors themselves had sponsored the project.

The working group members who were involved from the start in 1992 concluded that the first mission was accomplished after a study visit to Austria, where the Kisten-Pool system actors were visited. (Kisten-Pool is an application case discussed in Chapter 7.)

At an early stage, after the trip to Austria, and as soon as the group had convinced itself of the potentials of a national pool system, it was decided to plan and perform a large-scale pilot test. The purpose of this test was not to try out different tray and pallet designs, but to test and evaluate the pool *system* from logistical, economic, ergonomical and environmental perspectives. This was the second mission, and the most cost- and time-consuming part of this phase of the process.

During the pilot test phase, the working group decided to start looking at the design of an administrative concept for the pool system, but this mission was postponed, and taken up again in 1998, as the eighth and last mission.

It must be mentioned that, at this stage, the first working group looked at both trays and pallets. The need for a new type of returnable pallet was actually one of the main triggers for several of the working group members to join the process. For this reason, the working group decided in 1993 to design a material-neutral functional standard for half-pallets (800 by 600 millimetre footprint), to become a European standard. This mission was completed by the end of 1994.

The fifth and final mission of the first working group was started in early 1994, as a new sponsor, the Swedish Board of Agriculture, entered the scene. Sweden was soon going to become a member of the European Union, and the agricultural sector was facing a totally new market situation, where the open European market was identified as both a threat and an opportunity. The Board asked for a concept design of a pool system for returnable trays for vegetables. The report was delivered by the end of 1994, clearly showing the potential for a pool system.

Early agreement on some system and packaging parameters

After the large-scale pilot tests, the working group agreed on a number of system and product requirements. On the system level, it was decided that the actors wanted an open-loop pool system, open for all suppliers, wholesalers and retailers to become accepted as pool system members. All members of the working group were clear on the need for a neutral pool system solution that would not interfere with normal commercial competition. The pool system design would be deposit-based in order to achieve a high circulation speed and reduce loss of trays, already mentioned as two of the key parameters for pool system total economy.

There was also full unity behind the conclusion that no one desired a third-party operator to run the pool system solution. The reason for this was that all actors wanted to keep full control on system cost and future development issues.

Finally, the search for a suitable technology for the cleaning of used crates was identified as a high-priority system requirement. This had been identified during the study visit to Austria, where the cleaning of used trays was still an unsolved issue in 1992.

It was concluded at an early stage that both trays and pallets would follow the European pallet standard and its modules. Tray footprint outer dimensions were defined as 600 by 400 millimetres. The tray would be based on 100 per cent recyclable thermoplastics (HDPE or PP), designed with stack/nest functions based on 180-degree rotation of trays. This was considered the optimal way of reducing the space requirements for the return handling and transport of empty trays. Other design solutions for space reduction of empty trays were turned down: no foldable/collapsible or bale-arm stack/nest trays because of the bad quality of existing trays (eg hinges) and hygiene (difficulties in cleaning).

The first working group was closed at the beginning of 1995, when the logistics manager at the largest retailer in Sweden stopped the vegetable growers from taking the initiative in starting and driving the development of a packaging pool, an option opened while working on mission 5.

Working Group 2, 1995–99

Two new working groups, one for trays and one for pallets, were formed during 1995 as a result of a common initiative by the suppliers and the retailers. When Working Group 2 was formed in 1995, new group members were invited into the process. Knowledge continuity was secured, as three of the members from the first working group became members of the second group. The study visit strategy in mission 1 was repeated.

Three missions were accomplished by Working Group 2. The first mission was the most time-consuming and effort-demanding of all eight missions. The working group was asked by the suppliers and the retailers to develop a specification of requirements on a business-wide, returnable tray, followed by a tender process (1995–98).

The second mission was to perform an environmental evaluation of a plastic tray (1996–97), and the third mission was taken up from the first working group, how to design an administrative concept for the pool system and establish a member-owned pool company (1998–99).

The mission of developing a specification of requirements and undertaking a tender process has been selected here for an in-depth description and analysis, as it provides the basis for the description of how multi-party cooperation concerning change management, learning, reaching consensus and decision making has been managed in this process. In 1995–96, two conflicting parties were identified. The suppliers of meat and cured meats, poultry and delicatessen stood against the suppliers of fruits and vegetables. These two parties continued to fight for their own interests throughout the process.

The issue that the two groups had difficulty agreeing on was whether the trays should be ventilated/drained or closed. The design of handles, perforated or non-perforated, was also much discussed. Another hot topic, repeatedly being put on the agenda, was the debate on tray height dimensions. Discussion on which colour should be chosen for the trays was also often on the agenda, causing conflicting views.

The working group identified two questions to be carefully considered when deciding on tray properties: which of these two groups has the most urgent need/use of a common tray? And which of these two businesses has the largest volume?

Certain issues were covered repeatedly or deliberately postponed. The decision making was based on a negotiation- and majority-based consensus decision strategy. This was time-consuming. The definition of tray heights is one example of this. At a working group meeting during a study trip to Finland in August 1996, it was decided to start a project to test how the most frequent products would fit into different tray heights. First, a test protocol was compiled. During October 1996, a large number of test packing operations took place all over Sweden. More than 200 different frequent products were included in the test. In order to achieve a unified height on loaded pallets, as well as acceptable fill rates, the following three heights were proposed and decided upon in November: 110, 140 and 165 millimetres.

The 'U-turn'

In May 1997, one group member came back from a trade fair in Brussels, where he had seen a new type of tray with interesting properties. This was the second-generation bale-arm tray developed by Tesco. The empty nesting space reduction capacity was an impressive 75 per cent, to be compared with the 50–55 per cent offered by the 180-degree rotation stack/nest trays. This parameter, *empty tray space reduction*, had not been in focus earlier in the development process, since the working group had decided on the 180-degree rotation stack/nest tray concept, excluding other space reduction solutions for quality and hygienic reasons. The Tesco tray soon gained high appeal from the retailers' point of view, thanks to its space reduction features. Now the process entered into what is described as 'the U-turn' by four of the group members. Or, as another member described it, 'it went from evolution to revolution'.

The second half of 1997 and 1998 were turbulent times, as the retailers formed their argumentation for the Tesco crate while the meat industry together with other suppliers fought for their positions, which had been formally agreed upon in the working group's specification of requirements for a returnable tray. The working group members concluded that lots of action took place behind the scene during the final stages of this process.

In May 1999, the pool system company was finally provided with the investment capital required for concluding the contracts concerning pallets and trays. The Tesco tray supplier was selected as supplier to the pool system. During 2000, the first trays were introduced in the market. It can be noted that the heights of the trays in operation today are somewhat different from those decided after the large packing test in 1996 (in brackets): 199 (165), 167 (140) and 106 (110) millimetres.

Discussion and conclusions

The first mission in 1992 (repeated in 1995) was critical in order to reach a common vision within the working groups. The importance of ensuring that all players in a change process share the same vision has been pointed out by both Kanter (1984) and Sarv and Landborn (2003). As this mission was in part repeated when Working Group 2 was started, the new members could be introduced and enabled to share the vision of the process. Study visits – both abroad and within the national supply chains – and large-scale pilot tests have been identified as the most efficient methods of acquiring new knowledge on packaging and logistics.

All working group members comment on the time-consuming nature of the process. At the same time they conclude that future development of packaging and logistics systems must be based on cooperation and an active dialogue between the actors along a supply chain. Lee *et al* (1995) point out the importance of having a 'dominant designer' who pushes the development by making the proper decisions. In a Dutch case described by Koehorst, de Vries and Wubben (1999), the large retailer Albert Heijn and the packaging company Wavin are defined as dominant designers (this case is considered in Chapter 7). This is confirmed by the earlier case study, which described how Tesco managed to develop and implement its second-generation bale-arm tray within two years. The suppliers had little opportunity to influence tray design in both these cases. In the Swedish case, a more time-consuming process, all the actors had the opportunity to argue for their interest in cooperation with the other actors, who could accept their proposals on specific design issues.

The early closing of certain design parameters was a reason for the 'U-turn' turbulence late in the decision process. The first working group had decided to exclude the bale-arm tray design for quality and hygienic reasons. This has been commented upon in Stahre (1996), where he describes Safeway's high loss of trays due to weak material in the bale arms. That was a material technology problem, which was solved when Tesco developed its second-generation bale-arm tray.

By focusing on the stack/nest design based on 180-degree rotation, both working groups *missed* that product development had advanced during the years. The possibility of improving the empty tray space reduction capacity by looking at new developments was neglected. Not until a late stage was the new second-generation bale-arm tray with a considerably better space reduction capacity introduced by the retailers. Hygienic aspects could still be raised against this tray design, but the bale-arm quality problems had been solved since the initial decision in 1993 to exclude this tray design.

Two patterns can be identified on how difficult issues were solved within the second working group. The first pattern shows how tricky questions were postponed, in some cases more than twice, in order to be solved later on in the process. Certain issues had to be taken off the agenda, since too much attention and time were given to aspects that could be defined as secondary (eg choice of colour of trays). A second pattern used to solve certain issues was pilot tests or internal investigations within group members' own organizations (eg test packing of the 200 most frequent products to define tray heights, or performing other tests with closed and perforated trays).

Four conclusions can be presented. They point at general management issues that can be applied to any type of development or change process. However, it must be stressed that the logisticians who were involved in this development process were not fully aware of the impact of these prerequisites.

First, the management of the initial process is of utmost importance: the forming of a common objective, or a commonly shared vision, that all participants wish to reach. In this case the commonly shared vision was to obtain logistical efficiency enhancement, including an understanding of the impact of applying a supply chain total cost savings perspective.

The second conclusion is the importance of creating a common understanding within a development project and its working groups, as well as a common knowledge platform, upon which new knowledge can be successively added. Study visits, domestic as well as abroad, proved to be an efficient tool to create both common knowledge and better group dynamics.

The third conclusion points to the need to establish transparency throughout the pool system. This is an important factor, enabling pool members to see where costs and savings come up. Transparency provides better understanding of which actions need to be taken to improve system properties. Transparency is an important aspect when parties sit down to ordinary commercial negotiations on prices and terms, as cost and savings imbalances caused by the returnable packaging system must be adjusted there.

Finally, the fourth conclusion is that this type of development and decision process must include other professional specialists. The working group members – more or less all logisticians – pointed out the need to include professional skill from the commercial departments at their companies, both procurement and sales, into the preparation work within the decision process. This would probably have facilitated the forthcoming implementation of the pool system.

The concluding message is that customers of the packaging industry must establish good, long-term relations with packaging industry experts in order to keep up with product development. By doing that, it would be possible to avoid traumatic final stages as in the Swedish process.

It should also be noted that, by 2004, product development within returnable transport packaging was showing that the foldable/collapsible trays were the growing part of returnable transport packaging. This type of tray accounts for 150 million of a total of 275 million returnable trays now being used in Europe (Arca Systems AB, 2004). In only one year, 2002–03, the number of foldable trays increased by 15–20 million. There are also some 90 million rigid and stack/nest trays in circulation and some 35 million bale-arm trays. Neither of these two types of tray shows any increase in use.

SUMMARY AND CONCLUSIONS

A full discussion of the key learning points in terms of the packaging logistics decision matrix will be undertaken in Chapter 8 after the application case studies have been presented in the next chapter. At this stage therefore only a summary of these issues is required. Table 6.2 attempts to provide a summary of the contrasts between both cases and from this identify some of the 'lessons' for later discussion. It is important to note that no personal criticism is intended by this contrast. Organizations and individuals found themselves in a set of situations and circumstances and acted in the ways they felt appropriate. The 'lessons' are drawn to raise (self-)awareness of the potential issues for tackling change in such circumstances.

The most obvious difference between the two cases is the pace of development, being very much more rapid in the UK. This pace stems from the direction given to the process by Tesco and in particular its high board-level interest. This was added to by the involvement of a multifunctional aspect to the process, stemming from internal and external (supplier) involvement. In Sweden the process was more passive and less directive and organizations, whilst perhaps having greater group dynamics, tended to revert to their own organizational

Table 6.2 Issues from the major case studies

	UK Case	Swedish Case
Pace of development	Rapid development period, two years.	Slower development period, eight years.
Top management approach	Driven by Tesco board as a business priority.	Management support from companies, but essentially passive.
Importance of logistics	Board-level priority.	Not on the agenda at board level.
Functional approach	Logistics and supply chain orientation, so multifunctional teams introduced.	Some multifunctional components, but mainly separate identities maintained.
Awareness of technology	Technological improvements demanded to 'fix' problems.	Acceptance of current technological state.
Group dynamics	Imposition by Tesco, but some dynamic 'following' – industry as a whole came into line later.	Good working group and study tour dynamics. Being involved and learning together encouraged interactions. Wider discussions ensued.

requirements. Perhaps surprisingly, this pace was not adversely affected in the UK by an unwillingness to accept the current technological situation. Technological solutions were demanded to 'fix' problems, yet this did not seem to delay the process. In Sweden, by contrast, initial acceptance of supposed limits to technology closed off debate and choice, but did not speed up the process. In essence, the pace of the solution was determined by a clear dominant force having the power and vision to seek rapid solutions. This vision extended to the supply chain as a whole as opposed to being limited simply to company-specific solutions. The process in the UK was opportunity-driven rather than problem-oriented as in Sweden.

7

Application Case Studies

The major case studies discussed in the previous chapter provide contrasting approaches to packaging logistics change and problem solutions. In this chapter, 10 smaller application case studies are used to illustrate different aspects of managing change and finding solutions in the broad area of packaging logistics. As before, there is no intention of suggesting that any of these cases are 'right' or 'wrong'; rather the aim is to explore aspects of change implementation and business practice.

The cases have been selected in a variety of ways. Some involve situations with which the authors have been intimately involved. These in particular build on the major case studies in the last chapter. Others are drawn from research activities and management development programmes conducted as part of ongoing activities by the authors. Still more have been produced by summarizing material that is found in the literature. These are not intended to be exhaustive case studies but rather are indicative of the issues and the solutions that may be found in the real world. Table 7.1 provides some basic brief descriptions of the cases.

Table 7.1   Application case studies – introduction

Title of Case		Issue
A	Kisten-Pool, Austria	The introduction of reusable containers for vegetables.
B	Versfust Project, Netherlands	The introduction of a standard returnable crate for food products.
C	Tine Milk, Norway	The development of a roll-rack for movement of milk direct to the shop floor.
D	Packaging development in FMCG, Sweden	Testing of shop-ready merchandise on pallets.
E	Packaging and display, Sweden	Testing of two types of packaging and display units.
F	Fresh fruit salad packaging for airfreight, South Africa and UK	The redesign of packaging for aircraft transport.
G	Packaging for air cargo, South Africa and UK	Issues in temperature controlled supply chains given global time-control sourcing.
H	Mercadona, Spain	Handling systems in a fast-growing regional supermarket chain.
I	Sainsbury – from cans to cartons, UK	Logistics implications of changing packaging shapes and types.
J	Reusable plastic containers, California	A field trial of the use of plastic containers for fresh food products.

CASE A: KISTEN-POOL, AUSTRIA

Kisten-Pool is an early case illustration of the potential for reusable containers. Austrian fruit and vegetable growers, in active cooperation with government authorities, created a simple and efficient system for reusable vegetable containers. This system (known as the Kisten-Pool – 'the reusable container pool') reduced substantially the annual need for 25 million disposable containers and drastically reduced packaging costs.

Background

In 1988 the Austrian Department of Agriculture launched a study on the economies of reusable containers. This study showed that there were financial benefits to be gained with reusable containers. However, no changes resulted directly from the study. At the end of 1988, the growers' Marktbüro für Obst und Gemüse (market organization for fruit and vegetables) called a meeting of all parties involved, including the government, where the basis for a pilot project was discussed.

Rapid shift from test to operation

The parties quickly agreed to start a test with 100,000 containers. Production of these containers was completed by 1 July 1989, and they went into immediate use. The government contributed one-third of the cost of the containers. During the autumn and winter of 1989–90, the College of Agriculture undertook an economic study and evaluated the pilot project in terms of modifications in the system and the design of containers. The pilot project worked out so well that retailers decided to use the containers even before the College of Agriculture had completed their evaluation. The use of containers kept increasing, although at this stage the system operated essentially without any rules. By 1 July 1990, however, the parties involved had drafted rules for how the Kisten-Pool should work.

The pool operated as a non-profit association. Anyone handling fruit and vegetables was entitled to become a member. A new member signed an agreement to follow the Kisten-Pool rules, purchase containers and pay for each purchased container to the Kisten-Pool. The members then used as many of the containers in the system as they wanted. The packaging company supplied containers, and the purchaser was obliged to inform the Kisten-Pool about all purchases of new containers. Members could choose to exchange containers on a one-for-one basis or to pay a deposit per container.

The impact on various wholesalers has been somewhat different. By the early 1990s, 30 per cent of Konsum's handling of fruit and vegetables was in reusable containers. BILLA, a major distributor and supermarket chain, switched entirely to the reusable containers. Even imported goods were repacked in the reusable containers.

LGV, one of Austria's biggest distributors of vegetables and fruit, in parallel with the reusable containers handled seven types of disposable boxes. Depending on the customer's wishes, peppers (paprika), for instance, were packed in eight different types of containers! This was, of course, an untenable situation for LGV. It took six to eight people to repack vegetables in order to deliver them to the customer in the desired packaging. Simplification and standardization were necessary in such a situation.

Quality improvement

According to BILLA (the shop chain), each of their containers made an average of 30 trips a year to growers and shops. Naturally, economic benefits played a major role. It is obvious that financial improvements were among the decisive factors in BILLA's decision to join the Kisten-Pool, but the quality aspects were also of great importance. Growers used to force 20–22 heads of lettuce into a cardboard carton to keep packaging costs down. Instead, 12–14 heads of lettuce were placed in a reusable container and the consumer was offered a higher-quality, more attractive product. There was far less damaged fruit and vegetables thanks to the containers – which was also a profitability factor. BILLA introduced a debit/credit system for the containers with suppliers, but exchanged one for one whenever possible.

Source: Author interviews.

CASE B: VERSFUST PROJECT, NETHERLANDS

Albert Heijn is a Dutch supermarket chain and part of the international food retailer Ahold. Until 1994, fresh foods were supplied to Albert Heijn in a wide variety of crates. The varied crates could not be stacked. Crates for return had to remain in storage until suppliers came to collect them. In 1994, the company took the decision to develop a new logistics concept based on a modular approach to crate sizes and multi-product usage. In cooperation with crate manufacturer Wavin, Albert Heijn developed the specifications for a standard crate concept: the 'freshcrate'.

The idea behind the freshcrate was that it would offer the potential to cut costs throughout the supply chain by simplifying the exchange between the company's various outlets and its fresh food suppliers. It presented the potential to create more space, as the new standard crates would easily stack and this in turn would simplify and speed up the supplier's collection of used crates.

Freshcrate development: technical specifications

At the early stages of the freshcrate's development, Albert Heijn and Wavin determined the crate's technical specifications. They developed the crate design knowing that it would have to be acceptable to *all* parties involved in the logistics process, be suitable for a large array of fresh foods and be suitable for either packaged or unpackaged foods.

Ultimately, however, whilst acknowledging the importance of the other parties from the onset, it was this two-company coalition that determined the freshcrate's technical specifications. All companies wishing to become involved in the concept in the future would have to adhere to the creators' specifications. The technical specifications, as agreed by Albert Heijn and Wavin, are:

- *To minimize wasted or idle space within the crates.* Crate sizes were selected from the preference range developed by the Dutch Foundation 'Collomoduul', a modular system for the packaging of food products. Inner sizes were fixed and two different heights were made available.

- *To minimize wasted or idle space in transporting the crates.* Outer sizes were fixed to be compatible with standard pallets and to be used on standard conveyor belts.

- *To assist with handling of the crates, protect crate content and facilitate easy cleaning of the crates.* The edges and angles were designed to be smooth.

- *To be hygienic.* The crate's material must not affect the crate's content.

- *To accommodate various users.* The crates had to be easy to fill using either manual or automated systems.

- *To assist with the flow of information.* There had to be a facility for displaying crate identification, such as a bar code.

- *To maximize use of the crates.* Crates had to be presentable enough to be placed on the retailer's shop floor.

- *To reduce used crate storage space.* Crates had to stack easily.

Crate sizes complied with Dutch standards only and not with pan-European standards. There were also legal requirements and other binding agreements, including European Packaging Directives and Dutch packaging covenants.

Further development of the freshcrate concept: coordination

Although initiated by Albert Heijn, further development of the concept required the involvement and cooperation of many parties –

producers, manufacturers and retailers. Albert Heijn, along with an organization representing Dutch retailers (the Central Bureau of Food Trade) and an organization representing a large group of branded products producers (the Brand Article Foundation), formed the Freshcrate Foundation to take responsibility for decision-making processes and continuity issues. Primary tasks included the setting of tariffs, development and implementation of policy, controlling of rights and coordination of communications. The Foundation was also responsible for charting and following new developments. The Freshcrate Foundation introduced the standard crate in a three-phased project plan called 'Nationaal Versfust: a new logistics concept for the fresh food chain'.

The pilot phase

The pilot phase was designed to test whether the right technical and organizational choices had been made. In technical terms, the pilot phase revealed that the two-height option did not accommodate all necessary products. An additional two heights were made available, along with a 'semi-crate', which offered a reduced width. A large number of fresh food suppliers reported benefits with the freshcrates. The use of a standard crate removed the need for many suppliers to use a number of different crate systems. The transition to the new standard crate appeared most problematic for companies that formerly shipped goods in cardboard boxes, as they were required to alter their handling procedures. However, the majority of super-markets reported a big improvement following the introduction of the standard crate.

In practical, organizational terms, the pilot phase identified a number of day-to-day problems concerning management systems, user structures and pool arrangements. These issues were addressed by *all* parties and, as a result, both retailers and producers became involved in the evolution of the freshcrate concept. Their involvement heightened commitment to the project.

The pilot phase revealed that, whilst the benefits of the new crate varied, two emerging issues needed to be examined. First, further examination was required into producers that were still using the old one-time non-reusable packaging and were potentially facing substantial conversion problems. Secondly, there was still relatively little insight into the optimum system of returning and cleaning the crates.

Phases two and three

The second phase commenced with the freshcrate operating on a much larger scale and competing with foreign crate systems. Although not by design, the Dutch crate matches other international standards for crates, pallets, lorries and containers, thus broadening the product's appeal. The initial target was to produce a minimum of 4 million crates within three years. The first 18 months of the project led to the use of 6 million crates. The increase in the number of freshcrates also impacted upon the overall number of crates in circulation, reducing this by 20 per cent. The third phase further investigated issues of logistics, information technology, quality and finance issues in the continued development of the system.

Lessons learnt

The introduction and general transition towards using the freshcrate drastically changed logistics management for the manufacturers and producers of fresh foods. Successes can be attributed to early cooperation between a large number of producers, manufacturers and retailers. Each was involved in the pilot phase to arrive at optimal specificity. However, companies still using non-reusable packaging perceived transition to the new system as problematic, citing investment costs and loss of existing installations as potentially detrimental. Indeed, research has shown that, for these businesses, costs as yet outweigh the financial benefits of the new system.

In practice, three key factors significantly influence the success of the freshcrate system: the availability of a sufficient number of empty and clean crates at the appropriate time; the efficiency of product transportation, which impacts upon crate dimensions, pallet sizes and vehicle capabilities; and the extent to which information can flow with, and independent of, the goods.

Source: This case was adapted by Pamela Bremner from: H Koehorst, H de Vries and E Wubben (1999) Standardisation of crates: lessons from the Versfust (Freshcrate) project, *Supply Chain Management*, 4 (2), pp 95–101. Copyright © MCB University Press. This material is republished with permission, Emerald Group Publishing Limited.

CASE C: TINE MILK, NORWAY

Tine is a farmer-owned cooperative; their core business is the development, production and distribution of dairy products. Tine's main product is fresh milk, distributed in 1-litre cartons. As the largest player in the Norwegian food market, the company generates an annual turnover of US $1.6 billion and employs approximately 5,300 employees. Unlike most other food manufacturers in Norway, Tine delivers its products directly to the stores. Enabling this direct delivery operation is the company's involvement in a distribution partnership, 'the Joint Agricultural Fresh Food Distribution'. This partnership with two other food manufacturers, Gilde and Prior, permits the transportation of Tine's products to each of Norway's 4,500 food outlets. The products are transported through common regional terminals. Each regional terminal is owned by one of the three partners.

The development of the roll-rack

Leading to the development of the roll-rack, a plastic crate was used to transport fresh milk products. The plastic crates had to be lifted into transportation vehicles, removed and placed into storage refrigerators at the retail outlet, and then products were removed from the crates and placed into display facilities on the retail outlet shop floor.

To reduce the amount of lifting and handling of the fresh milk product and to suit the overall logistics process better, both economically and environmentally, Tine developed the roll-rack. Tine's roll-rack is a metal construction, set on wheels, and is approximately 40 by 40 centimetres with a height of 67 centimetres. Designed to accommodate 160 1-litre cartons, it is a flexible construction in that, internally, it can be split into compartments of variable size and, externally, the front can be opened and widened so that other empty roll-racks can be inserted.

The roll-rack costs approximately US $280–430 per unit and, in normal circumstances, there are 80,000 in operation and a further 30,000 in stock. The roll-rack has become the dominant load carrier for fresh milk and is now also used for a selection of other products including other types of milk and juice.

Uses and benefits of the roll-rack

The roll-rack's uses and intended benefits are multifaceted. First, it is used to transport the product from Tine's distribution terminal to the transportation vehicle to the retailer's store. There is therefore only one loading operation of milk into the roll-rack and only one loading/ unloading of the roll-rack to and from the transportation vehicle. Furthermore, the roll-rack's wheels remove any need for lifting the crate throughout the process.

The roll-rack is then used to display the product within the store; the rack is placed in refrigerators on the shop floor, either placed there directly from the transportation vehicle or via the retailer's holding area. As before, the roll-rack's wheels remove any need for lifting the crate. The combined 'cradle to grave' storage and transportation of the product reduces the potential for damaging stock. The wide, open front of the crate makes it ideally suited to consumers' needs: they can easily select their product and can easily read product labelling information.

Finally, the empty roll-rack, when removed from the shop floor and returned to the distribution centre, is then used to store other empty racks, thus reducing return transportation space and consequently costs.

Limitations of the roll-rack

Whilst the roll-rack is capable of transporting products other than the dominant 1-litre fresh milk carton, there are approximately 1,000 Tine products that do require other types of carrier. These other carriers include plastic crates, cardboard boxes and pallets. Since the introduction of the roll-rack, Tine has adapted it to accommodate carriage of plastic troughs/trays within it by increasing the width by 1 centimetre, but a variety of other carriers are still used.

There are limitations even where the 1-litre fresh milk carton is concerned. Full use of the roll-rack requires suitable facilities at the consumer end of the transportation phase. Schools and canteens are examples of end users that do not have the space to store or display the crates, and they also do not order the volumes necessary to fill the roll-racks. A further concern for Tine's use of the roll-rack is the general reduction in 1-litre carton milk sales. With the introduction of many new products, Tine has experienced a reduction of milk sales as a percentage of all products within its distribution network.

Tine had developed an effective carrier for its main product, 1-litre fresh milk cartons. The benefits, although not universal, are economically and environmentally efficient. However, despite the roll-rack's flexible design, which can accommodate products other than those it was specifically designed for, many of Tine's other products are still not compatible with this form of carrier. Consideration must be given to how the roll-rack can be adapted to suit the network of products better.

CASE D: PACKAGING DEVELOPMENT IN FMCG, SWEDEN

In this case, a test unit combining sales packaging as well as secondary and tertiary packaging was developed by a leading package supplier for the FMCG industry and compared to a traditional half-sized standard Euro pallet.

The test unit is made of plastic and covered with a bottom sheet on which packages are placed on top of each other in cardboard layers. The unit format is that of a quarter-sized standard Euro pallet. The specification of the test unit was based on requirements throughout the value chain from the packaging supplier's customers to the end consumers. A unique solution was created, intended to consider requirements from more than one part of the value chain. The test unit was compared with a half-sized standard Euro pallet where the packages were packed in secondary packaging and then were stacked on the pallet. The impact on sales, system integration, infrastructure dynamics and cost-versus-value on the whole value chain was studied.

One of the studies undertaken was the value rating in the retail store based on 100 consumer interviews. It was carried out in a Swedish retail outlet where the test unit was displayed and evaluated at two different locations in the store, one in the open sales area (the market-place) and the other in the traditional shelf space. In conjunction with this qualitative research, quantitative studies were undertaken in Estonia, the United Kingdom, Sweden and Russia. In each country, already-established products were displayed in the test unit and the sales results were compared to sales in traditional secondary packages displayed on traditional shelf positions.

Results

The case was based on the combination of primary, secondary and tertiary packaging to develop a complete sales solution (test unit). The

Table 7.2   Handling time in seconds per litre

	Quarter-Sized Euro Pallet – the Test Unit	Trays on Standard Euro Pallet
Wholesaler	4.2	34.2
Retailer	4.8	35.0
Total	9.0	69.2

handling time for the unit was compared to handling of a traditional half-sized standard Euro pallet with standard tray secondary packaging. The case showed a decrease of 87 per cent in handling time in seconds per litre for the wholesaler and the retailer, as shown in Table 7.2. In addition, cardboard consumption was reduced by 65 per cent for the test unit as compared to that consumed by the standard pallet.

By placing the half-sized standard Euro pallet and the test unit in a Swedish retail outlet, at two alternative shop locations (the marketplace and ordinary shelf space), consumer perception in terms of accessibility, visibility, attractiveness and quality was validated through consumer interviews, with results as in Table 7.3.

Table 7.3   Average rating values of the units

Features	Marketplace		Shelf	
	Test Unit	Half Standard Euro Pallet	Test Unit	Half Standard Euro Pallet
Accessibility	6.4	3.8	6.1	4.9
Visibility	6.7	3.8	6.0	5.5
Attractiveness	6.2	3.5	5.5	5.3
Quality	5.2	3.3	4.4	4.9
Preferable Alternative	98%	2%	65%	35%

In conjunction with this research, quantitative studies on sales results were undertaken in a number of markets. The first case, in Estonia, showed an increase in sales of 16 per cent for the test unit compared to sales from standard trays on shelves. The second case included one of the major multinational retail chains based in the UK, where the products in the test unit increased in sales by 11 per cent compared to traditional sales in trays. In the third case, where a major international brand was evaluated in the test unit in Sweden, sales grew by 65 per cent compared to traditional sales in trays on half-sized standard Euro pallets. In the last case, in Russia, products on display in the test unit increased sales by 15 per cent. The results from these four cases strongly underscore that consumers prefer the test unit mode.

Impacts

From the *manufacturer* perspective in using the test unit, several implications were found. First, the manufacturer had to invest in a new packaging line in order to handle this unit efficiently. Hand-packing can of course be viable at the start, but, if sales take off as indicated, automation is inevitable. This will incur a higher product cost due to equipment investment. On the other hand, reduced use of cardboard material in production and an increase in sales volume, due to increased communication, customer value and convenience, will allow depreciation of that investment.

Another and more difficult implication to resolve is the use of quarter-sized standard Euro pallets. Much of the infrastructure in handling food products is built around full-size pallets where half-modules can relatively easily be handled, since forklifts and other systems such as pallet racking can be utilized. When it comes to the quarter-sized Euro pallet there has to be a separate set-up. As one example, the quarter-sized Euro pallet has to be stored on a slave pallet, normally a full-sized Euro pallet. This will make the height of the unit too high to place in the normal pallet racking system, which leads to less package layers on the pallet, resulting in a lower packaging efficiency.

The same type of complication as for the manufacturer is valid for any party in the value chain, such as the *wholesaler*, that is storing products on pallets. Physical handling is also more complicated due to low flexibility on the forklifts, ie the distance between the forks. The quarter-sized Euro pallet demands flexibility to avoid instability. In addition, such instability caused by the format of the pallet will have negative impact in terms of higher risks of package damage in transportation and handling. This demands special systems for fixation in transport and handling, which is another infrastructure investment to be made. One positive effect of the test unit is the lower frequency and volume of single-tray order picking, which leads to higher customer value in terms of lower personnel requirements and also convenience in handling packages. Less handling of the package will yield a higher-quality package to the end consumer, and hence increased customer value.

From a *retail* point of view, the test unit is convenient, and easy to locate and handle due to its size and format. Enhanced communication and customer value are achieved through enabling flexible location and attractive product variations. On the other hand, handling becomes almost impossible if no adequate handling equipment is available. The forklifts used in stores are very often less flexible than those used in warehouses. If the test unit is being delivered on a slave pallet to accommodate better handling for upstream actors in the value chain, the result may be unresolvable problems for a retail store that rarely has the facilities to unload a pallet from a slave pallet.

Conclusions

When looking into the situation, it is clear that changing store presentation for the product will drive consumer interest and purchase, and consequently strengthen the brand and open up opportunities for market share increase. The consumer value also incurs a market share and volume increase; however, the cost in terms of investments and handling may reduce the effects of such an increase.

- *Cost influence.* A change in the packaging system will incur increased costs in terms of new investments. However, these can be balanced through increase in sales, fewer personnel or less use of packaging material.

- *Convenience influence.* The proposed test unit enhances convenience to the end consumer, which leads to an increase in sales. This positive effect may, however, cause less convenience for other actors in the value chain in terms of deviation from the standard pallet system.

- *Customer value influence.* The case shows a change in the perceived customer value for some actors, such as the consumers and to some extent the retailer. There is, however, a trade-off in the deviation from standard pallets.

- *Communication influence.* The case shows an increased possibility of more efficient communication to the end consumer, and thus an increase in sales.

The case shows impact on and trade-offs in packaging efficiency for the different value chain actors. The positive effects of brand advertising have been demonstrated. However, they may not compensate for less efficient packaging. The market need will easily be affected and turn into a higher supply chain push when creating packaging solutions that will attract retail outlets as well as consumers. However, it is important to take a systems approach and evaluate the whole supply chain efficiency from both the packaging and the logistics point of view.

Source: This case was adapted by Gunilla Jönson and Leigh Sparks from: A Olsson and M Györei (2002) Packaging through the value chain in the customer perspective marketing mix, *Packaging Technology and Science*, 15, pp 231–39. Copyright © 2002 John Wiley & Sons Limited. This material is republished with permission of John Wiley & Sons Limited.

CASE E: PACKAGING AND DISPLAY, SWEDEN

An FMCG product was sold through two different kinds of display units, one ready-made display pallet and one alternative display unit. Unit A was a half-sized standard Euro pallet (400 by 600 millimetres) delivered directly to the display area. Only the cover had to be removed, and it was then used as part of the display. Unit B also had all material delivered on the pallet. However, the delivery had to be dismantled and then erected at the point of display.

The impact of the two different displays, in terms of packaging, brand advertising, and sales in competition with other brands, as well as the sales impact, was measured in a study that was undertaken in 10 retail outlets during a period of 26 weeks. Traditionally the product is displayed on the shelves using normal sales units.

First, display unit A was introduced in combination with a two-week TV advertising campaign on national channels. After another two weeks of using the display with no other advertising, the display unit was removed, and all sales went through the normal shelving position again. After a total of 14 weeks, ie six weeks after the removal of the first display unit, display unit B was introduced. This second display unit was similarly removed after a four-week period and all sales were reintroduced through the normal shelving position.

In order to study the impact of the whole subcategory of products, the case started with a four-week index period from the actual sales in the normal shelving position, where the index was set at 100 to enable comparison between the coming activities. The retail outlets used fixed prices and everyday low prices with yearly adjustments, and the price fluctuation was 0 per cent throughout the 26 weeks the tests were carried out.

Results

An increase in sales share for the tested brand and a decrease for the main competitor were noticed after introduction and a two-week TV advertisement of the display unit A (see Figure 7.1). However, these tendencies balanced out after a few weeks, and the sales shares went back to approximately the same level as before the unit was introduced. Even after the introduction of the display unit B, the market reaction faded after a few weeks, though not all the way back to the original sales share level. Three months after the introduction, the sales share of the tested brand was at a level equal to that of the main competitor. The third brand, ie the second competitor, was basically unaffected by the introductions. It should be mentioned that the third brand is mainly perceived by most people as an import and of inferior quality.

The really interesting finding comes when considering not only the sales share impact for different brands but also the total sales for this subcategory of products. In the first period of four weeks, sales equalled the index of 100. In the second period, when the display unit A was used, the index scored 111. In the third period, when no display units at all were used, the index scored 99. In the fourth period, when the display unit B was used, the index amounted to 124. Finally, the fifth period

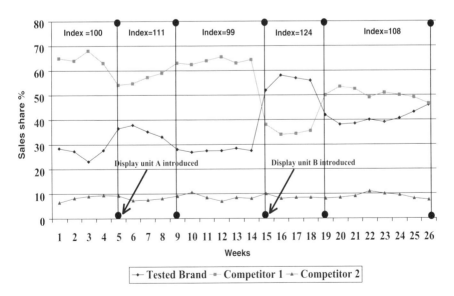

Figure 7.1   *Sales share (percentage) and subcategory sales index in 10 retail outlets*

index was at 108. The result shows an overall increase in actual sales for the subcategory in total, even if the sales share strengths for the two leading brands changed quite drastically. Compared to the national market, the subcategory did not develop at all according to what can be seen in this case. For the 26-week period, the index on the national market showed 97.

The impact on communication

The TV advertising in the second period (see Figure 7.1), together with the display unit A, might not have got the right impact due to the display design. The display's construction does not give full visibility of the product, which indicates communication inefficiency. With or without the TV advertisement, the communication provided by the second display (unit B) has a clear sales impact (see Figure 7.1).

The impact on production

In this case there was a low level of automation, but initiatives had been taken to find an automated solution for the display pallet package (unit A). If that was done, efficiency would increase for the display pallet solution, but not necessarily for the overall packaging operation of this product. Optimizing using the display unit B would increase the utilization of the existing automated line since more volume would run through one type of packaging operation. Cost savings would be made due to simplified material sourcing, adding convenience and customer value to the value chain, since a first-in-first-out principle would be more easily achieved. The internal handling for the manufacturer would be simplified with only one type of package for the product. For an external perspective of the manufacturer, the sales process could also be simplified using unit B, since its sales representatives could focus on selling one type of product concept rather than two, driving cost efficiency and simplified communication.

The impact on pricing

More stringent pricing, due to only one type of packaging option, would pave the way for margin improvements, since many wholesalers and distributors required pallet discounts on display A. Standardizing the product and decreasing the variety always involve a risk of losing value chain airtime, meaning that one product is equal to a certain time of discussion and shelf space, while two products will not double the time or shelf space, but will create more discussions than are required for just one product. This may be defensible if the result in financial terms is greater, but from a manufacturer-competitive perspective it might act as a strong barrier to competitor entry in the product segment.

The impact on the wholesaler

Changing perspective from the manufacturer to the wholesaler or distributor shows that there are other positive as well as negative effects. Wholesalers and distributors have mainly built up an infrastructure around full-sized Euro pallets (or the equivalent) so the display unit A can be handled, but not as efficiently and conveniently as a full-sized Euro pallet. On the other hand, the unit can reduce single-package order picking if the order to the retail outlet equals the volume of the display package, which gives increased customer value and convenience to the wholesaler and retailer. In that sense the unit will lower the handling cost. The system cost will be higher for the wholesaler/distributor because of dual package types for the same product. Sourcing and storing as well as system handling will be more complicated, and the previous risk also appears here, where first-in-last-out might occur. The capital tied up in stock will consequently be higher. The display unit B will therefore generate a lower cost, considering that only one type of packaging is used, and hence the higher cost for more unit-order picking.

The impact on the retailer

The retailer will also experience impacts due to the different characteristics of the display units. The unit A offers an easy solution for store placement, while the unit B demands more handling at set-up, thus creating differences in communication and customer value. On the other hand, the display unit A has low consumer visibility and accessibility, which requires more attendance by store personnel due to less communication impact, less customer value for both retail and consumer and less convenience for consumers. Furthermore, there will be the risk of driving the cost in a less beneficial manner. In many markets the store attendance work task is required from the manufacturer by the retailer, which will increase the cost significantly for the whole value chain, considering payment level and expenses incurred in moving merchandising people from store to store.

The impact on the consumer

Display unit A gives a rather confused impression from a consumer point of view. What is on offer? Considering the product perception from a consumer point of view, the two alternative display units position the product quite differently in terms of convenience, communication and customer value. From a value chain perspective, the two alternatives perform quite differently in their different transitions in the value chain, considering cost, communication, customer value and convenience.

Conclusions

The case shows that the type of packaging used will influence the retail sales as well as the whole supply chain in different ways:

- *Cost influence.* A change in the packaging system will incur increased costs in terms of new investments. However, these can be balanced through either an increase in sales, fewer personnel or less use of packaging material.

- *Convenience influence.* The proposed solutions enhance convenience to the end consumer, which leads to an increase in sales. This positive effect may, however, incur less convenience to other actors in the value chain in terms of more complicated handling.

- *Customer value influence.* There is a perceived customer value for the consumers and to some extent for the retailer. There is, however, a trade-off in handling at the retail level.

- *Communication influence.* There is an increased possibility of more efficient communication to the end consumer, and thus an increase in sales.

The market need will easily be affected and turn into a higher supply chain push when creating packaging solutions that will attract retail outlets as well as consumers. The study shows that packaging has the ability to change market position as well as market segment value. However, in this case the supply chain packaging efficiency is questioned, which indicates a need for changes in the supply handling to get a completely positive picture.

Source: This case was adapted by Gunilla Jönson and Leigh Sparks from: A Olsson and M Györei (2002) Packaging through the value chain in the customer perspective marketing mix, P*ackaging Technology and Science*, 15, pp 231–39. Copyright © 2002 John Wiley & Sons Limited. This material is republished with permission of John Wiley & Sons Limited.

CASE F: FRESH FRUIT SALAD PACKAGING FOR AIRFREIGHT, SOUTH AFRICA AND UK

Fresh fruit salad is fully prepared, ready to eat, in South Africa and flown overnight to the UK so that it is on the retail shelf the next day for consumers to select and consume. This demonstrates the span of control exercised by such retailers in the quality of preparation, presentation and delivery of a fragile product. It brings exotic products daily throughout the year across continents, products that would otherwise normally be absent for whole seasons.

In the high care section of the fresh fruit production unit, the component fruits such as pineapple, mango, melon, guava and papaya are prepared by removing their outer skins and other non-edible components. The remaining edible fresh fruit is then diced into smaller pieces that are easy to serve and consume immediately. The different varieties of fruit are then mixed together in punnet-sized consumer packs, normal clear plastic. These are then sealed with a film to protect the product throughout its journey to the end consumer. Each consumer pack is labelled. Throughout this process there is strict quality control to ensure that the flavour, sizing and trimming meet the retailer's standards.

Once outside the high care preparation area, the consumer packs are arranged in set quantities into transport boxes, which are normally cardboard. These transport boxes are labelled and sealed. The retail orders for these products are then arranged on to pallets according to their different destinations in the UK. Retailers have several distribution centres around the UK, and the correct quantity must go to each depot daily. These pallets are then labelled with their destination and other information.

So far, this production process is similar to that of many other products that a country produces for its own consumption. The next stage in the distribution channel is the transfer of the products from one continent to another by airfreight. Sometimes airfreight can be performed at a leisurely pace but, in the instance of the fresh fruit salad prepared in Johannesburg, South Africa, it is sent that same evening from Johannesburg airport by air cargo to Heathrow, London, where it arrives in the early hours of the morning (about 5 am). From Heathrow it is distributed to the various retailers' distribution centres that morning so that it can be on the retailers' shelves by the time consumers are leaving work to go home. They can collect their fresh fruit salad and eat it with the evening meal or snack on the way home.

Analysis and conclusions

The analysis of the case will cover two specific aspects: breathability of packaging and packaging design for improved space utilization.

Breathability is through the thin membrane film sealing the top of the consumer punnet pack containing the ready-to-eat fresh fruit salad. Some plants continue to live even after they have been harvested; a well-known instance is cut flowers. The packaging and the transport container have to allow the flow of vapours to escape. This applies to fresh fruit salad and is addressed by pores that are so tiny they are not visible. It has been known for fresh fruit salad packages to be placed upside down and the juices to leak out through these pores in the film. When this happens the product has to be thrown away.

The second aspect is packaging design for improved space utilization. As the fresh fruit salad is ready to eat, the weight of the product has already been reduced to a minimum when the skin and non-edible parts were removed during the production process. As well as reducing the actual weight in this way, it is also important to design the packaging so it is the minimum cube. In airfreight, both weight and cube impact on the cost of transportation, so it is worth examining those instances where there has been a redesign of the packaging to improve space utilization. In field research the author found out that the original design for the fresh fruit salad consumer pack was in the shape of a bowl. Clearly the marketing department thought that this was a useful shape because it looked like a small bowl from which people would normally eat a fruit salad. But this bowl design was not space efficient, although there is a need to be space efficient when using expensive airfreight. It was this bowl design, with one packed upside down on top of another to save space, that had the disastrous result of leakage and consequent product waste.

The packaging logistics redesign was a rectangular shape with a sloping base such that, by rotation of one pack by 180 degrees, it fitted on the bottom pack in a space-efficient way. By implementing this design at source, less space was needed for airfreight, the problem of leaking from upside-down bowls was eliminated and the packages did not need to be re-sorted in the UK prior to despatch to the retail distribution centres.

These cost savings created a better margin in retail for this premium product. It also enabled the retailer to range the fresh fruit salad offer in many other stores where previously the profit would have been marginal. In this way a change in packaging logistics design contributed directly to an increase in the growth in the demand for the ready-to-eat fresh fruit salad from South Africa.

The conclusion of this case study is that packaging logistics, correctly applied, is critical to the success of global sourcing of fresh ready-to-eat products that are transported by airfreight between the continent of origin and the continent of destination.

Source: Author interviews.

CASE G: PACKAGING FOR AIR CARGO, SOUTH AFRICA AND UK

A visit to the various types of fresh food departments in a modern supermarket will quickly reveal, by examining the country of origin, the wide range of products involved in daily overnight airfreight between continents. Daily sourcing has become global: mangetout from Zimbabwe, sugar snap peas from Kenya, blueberries from the United States, vegetables from Thailand, etc. What is not so visible to the consumer is the intense activity that takes place in packaging logistics and the strict temperature control regimes in airfreight to provide them with their choice of purchase.

The case study begins at the airport of the country of origin. The fieldwork took place in the airport of origin at Johannesburg, South Africa and at the airport of destination at Heathrow, London, UK. Operators have seen the results of low-quality packaging and poor temperature control. They also know how to achieve best practice through the application of the right packaging solutions for fresh products and how to maintain the strict temperature control disciplines that are so important for product freshness throughout the airfreight journey. These operators are located in the middle of the supply value channel. They do not control the suppliers' standards of packaging the fresh product. But they do see the contrasting results of good and bad practice. They also understand the demands of the fast pace of the fresh food global supply channel.

The case study starts with the fresh product arriving by temperature controlled road freight transport from the supplier into the air cargo fresh food transit facility operation at Johannesburg airport. This might be fresh fish from Namibia bound for Spain via Heathrow, London; fresh impala meat steaks from Zimbabwe; or fresh vegetables, cut flowers, ready-to-eat fresh fruit salad, etc from South Africa or neighbouring countries. The first checks made are that the product is at the correct temperature on arrival from the supplier and the product packaging is intact. There are two factors that can influence the product temperature on arrival. The first is the original temperature of the fresh product when it was prepared. If the fresh product was fruit or vegetables, a vital part of the harvesting process is removing the ground heat from the product before it is packaged and despatched. If the ground heat has not been removed then the product temperature will be too high. The refrigeration provided by transport vehicles is designed to maintain a cool temperature; it is not designed to remove ground heat from a hot product that is above its correct transport temperature. The second factor that can influence the product temperature on arrival is any infringement of the strict discipline of continuous and constant temperature control from the point of preparation and despatch. If, for example, the product was exposed to a high ambient temperature during despatch, then this could trigger the ripening process in fruit and vegetables that then generate heat of their own. This is one of the critical hazard points that needs to be checked in any temperature controlled supply chain.

As well as the normal international cargo paperwork procedures, fresh product requires special packaging for its intercontinental journey. This packaging has to be adequate for two extreme temperature conditions. The first is the very low temperatures that can exist during the flight itself in an aeroplane cargo hold, when the external temperature might be as low as –60 degrees. The cargo hold is not normally temperature controlled. The second is the very high temperatures that can exist out on the tarmac of a tropical airport while the product is standing, waiting to be loaded into the aeroplane cargo hold. These temperatures might rise to +40 degrees, the heat not only coming down from the sun but also up from the ground tarmac itself. The risk from these two temperature extremes can be very high, and extreme conditions are a severe challenge. So special measures have to be taken to isolate the fresh products from any exposure to high tarmac ground heat or the very cold surrounding during the flight itself.

There are solutions that good operators implement to protect their fresh product. The first is the investment in secondary packaging that has good properties for thermal protection. The second is the investment in special coverings that go around, over and under the product for the intercontinental portion of its journey. These special coverings are needed from the point of despatch from the airport of origin to the point of arrival at the airport of destination. They must be on the product before it goes out on to the tarmac ahead of being loaded into the aircraft and must stay on the product until it has been received into a temperature controlled reception warehouse at the airport of destination. These coverings are made from special fabric and foil. The specification that is required can be obtained from reputable operators that are experienced in implementing these solutions successfully. The failure to understand the temperature stresses of the air cargo segment of an intercontinental journey is a major pitfall for those suppliers who seek to save money by skimping on the secondary packaging for their fresh product or by ignoring the benefits of these specialist coverings. One operator has invested in mini refrigerated trailers that hold two pallets of fresh product each. These trailers are used to hold the product during despatch during the waiting and loading activities. The pallets are removed from the trailers only at the last moment, just as the aeroplane is loaded up. This investment guarantees a constant cool temperature for the product during this particularly vulnerable part of its journey.

At the airport of destination, Heathrow, London, UK, there is a specialist perishable cargo handling centre that has been set up by British Airways and is operated by a specialist temperature controlled logistics service provider. There are specially agreed swift procedures for these sensitive cargoes. The planes usually arrive early in the morning, about 5 am, after their overnight intercontinental flight. There are temperature controlled vehicles that go out to the arrival area of the aeroplane on landing. The containers of fresh product are loaded straight on to these vehicles and are brought back immediately to the temperature controlled reception area of the perishable cargo handling centre. In this way the product is back in a protected environment as quickly as possible.

Once inside the temperature controlled perishable cargo handling centre, there is a range of activities that can be conducted according to the service agreements with the customers. In the most straightforward agreement, the containers and pallets are moved directly from reception to despatch into the customer's temperature controlled vehicle (cross-docking). The centre provides the necessary clearance documentation so the product can be released to the customer. Other agreements may include a range of additional services. These services include: quality checking of the product on arrival; the physical separation of the product into the quantities required for different destinations, eg a retail customer may have several distribution centres in the UK; and labelling or even repackaging of the product. This is in addition to the full customs clearance process for all types of perishable cargo, including fresh meat.

It is inside the perishable cargo handling centre at Heathrow that it is possible to see the consequences of the application of different standards of packaging and the use of different insulation materials. Most products from Thailand come in polystyrene thermal boxes, which are very effective in preserving the quality of fresh product. Another effective practice is the use of thermal foil quilt covers that wrap around the whole pallet, sides, top and underneath; these keep the product fresh and greatly reduce the risk of product deterioration during its long-haul flight. There is also evidence of inappropriate or poor-quality packaging. Cardboard packaging is very weak when it gets wet and collapses. This moisture can come from the product when it is poorly insulated from the changes in temperature environments during the course of the air journey. Collapsed packaging can break open, with the consequent deterioration and loss of the fresh product. The supplier may have saved a few cents on the packaging but then lost many dollars or euros when the product itself has deteriorated. When a retailer rejects the supplier's product as unacceptable, there is the additional cost of the loss of profit at retail, empty shelves for the consumer and a possible long-term deterioration in the supplier–retailer relationship, with the risk of getting a bad reputation and loss of future orders. From this perspective, saving a few cents on proper thermal packaging materials, far from increasing the supplier's profit margin, can lead to a serious deterioration in the growth of the business. This was the single most forceful piece of advice given by logistics operators handling fresh product airfreight cargo.

Analysis and conclusions

The analysis of the case covers two points. The first is the importance of thermal insulation to protect fresh product from the extremes of high and low temperatures that can occur during intercontinental airfreight movements. The second is the very high risk to the market value of fresh product when suppliers use unsuitable, inferior packaging or even omit to wrap their fresh products with thermal foil covers on the sides, top and underneath. This is a lesson that all suppliers and those instructing suppliers need to take seriously.

The conclusion of this case study is that specialist thermal packaging logistics is critical to the success of using air cargo for the global sourcing of fresh products that are transported by aircraft between the continents of origin and of destination.

Source: Author interviews.

CASE H: MERCADONA, SPAIN

Mercadona (www.mercadona.es) is arguably the leading supermarket chain in Spain. It had almost 900 stores by the end of fiscal year 2004 and has a reputation as an innovative and rapidly growing successful business. To support its retail stores, Mercadona has focused on developing an effective and efficient supply chain with considerable investments in new distribution facilities, in-store presentation of products and new and refurbished store development.

A recently developed logistics centre is situated in the Granadilla de Abona industrial estate in the Canary Islands. The new logistics centre covers a surface area of 90,000 square metres, of which 42,000 square metres have been newly built for use as meat, fish, fruit and vegetables, frozen foods, refrigerated foods, non-perishable goods and packaging warehouses. This platform is equipped with the most modern technology for logistics centres, such as radio frequency. Likewise, automatic banding machines have been installed in order to reduce the heavy loads that workers would otherwise have to handle during packaging and pallet loading processes. Furthermore, a new generation press has been installed that optimizes recycling and management of the cardboard waste that the shops produce (230 tonnes/month), and also a washing conveyor for reusable boxes (240,000 boxes/month), all of which allows advances in the treatment and management of waste.

This logistics centre in Granadilla de Abona is Mercadona's sixth. It adds to the ones Mercadona currently has in Riba-Roja de Turia (Valencia), Antequera (Malaga), Sant Sadurni de Anoia (Barcelona), San Isidro (Alicante) and Huevar (Seville). All of these centres make up a network covering a surface area of 420,000 square metres, meaning that Mercadona can realistically expect to increase the efficiency of its supply chain.

One of the key points of difference in Mercadona is the prevalence of store-ready merchandising and the thought that has gone into the handling of products and their display at store level. As Figure 7.2

Figure 7.2 *Packaging and presentation in Mercadona* (Source: *author photographs, 2002 and 2003*)

Figure 7.2a

Figure 7.2b

Figure 7.2c

Figure 7.2d

Figure 7.2e

shows, there is a variety of types of packaging, both corrugated and plastic, used in the store. Handling systems are designed to allow easy movement.

RFID development

A further development (http://www.foodproductiondaily.com) has been the use of radio frequency identification (RFID) tags in its new Madrid logistics centre. These tags, developed by German firm Witron Logistik & Informatik, will be used to identify system pallets and help the retailer achieve complete traceability at a vital section of the supply chain. In the long term this should bring cost benefits due to less wastage and quicker identification of bottlenecks or weaknesses.

For the identification of system pallets – used for storing all incoming pallets in the goods-in area – Witron is using RFID tags integrated into each system pallet, rather than conventional bar-code labels. The company claims that this provides new benefits for Mercadona by increasing the reliability of the entire goods-in system. A scanning rate of almost 100 per cent and the long lifespan of the RFID tags used will result in quantifiable process advantages.

As far as Mercadona is concerned, all dry, fresh and frozen goods will be handled on the plastic system pallets. Mercadona's suppliers are currently using plastic pallets – without RFID tags for now – for the fresh and frozen goods areas (including meat as well as fruit and vegetables). In due course, by replacing worn-out plastic pallets with RFID tagged ones, there will be a gradual changeover from conventional plastic pallets to RFID system pallets within the fresh and frozen goods areas, which will result in fewer and fewer of the incoming goods having to be placed on system pallets. These system pallets will not only be used as an in-house transport device but will also be used within the entire supply chain. At present it is planned that the RFID tag will carry a 12-digit pallet number for clear identification purposes, and further information, such as the relevant product data, will be stored in the warehouse management system.

Source: Author fieldwork, www.mercadona.es, food productiondaily.com (2005). Original piece by Ahmed ElAmin (2005) Spanish retail achieves fresh fruit RFID traceability, http://www.foodproductiondaily.com/news/ng.asp?id= 59709, 29 April [accessed 24 October 2005]. Copyright © Decision News Media SAS. This material is republished with permission, Decision News Media.

CASE I: SAINSBURY – FROM CANS TO CARTONS, UK

In October 2004 Sainsbury finally got away from negative press stories in the UK with their announcement that they were switching some products from being sold in cans to making them available in cartons. Much was made of the 'death of the can' and of the consumer benefits to cartons, which were seen as the 'shape of the future'. The carton chosen was the Tetra Recart (www.tetrapak.com/uk/), which is a rectangular carton made out of paperboard laminate and designed for food products traditionally packed in cans, glass jars or pouches. Unlike tin cans, the cartons are made from a renewable resource and, as with tin cans, recycling will be possible. Figure 7.3 shows the changeover.

From the perspective of this book, however, the interesting aspect is the potential logistical benefits of this technological change. These are in some ways more economically, though perhaps less sociologically, interesting. Table 7.4 shows the significant data.

The new format is 12 per cent lighter and 30 per cent smaller than the can it replaces, but with almost the same contents. Because of this,

Figure 7.3   *The death of the tin can?* (Source: *author scans, 2004*)

Figure 7.3a

Figure 7.3b

Table 7.4   Dimensions of cans and cartons

		Tin Can	Carton	Percentage Change
Cubic Space:	can	477 cm³	421 cm³	−11.7
	cube	607 cm³	421 cm³	−30.6
Weight:	content	400g	390g	−2.5
	total	468g	412g	−12.0

the packing density is vastly improved and the weight can more easily fit into vehicles. Downsides might include the ability to maintain shape on pallet loads and possible consumer reaction during changeover.

A similar packaging initiative has been developed in the United States between Tetra Recart cartons and Hormel Foods Stagg Chilli. The Tetrapak USA website (www.tetrapakusa.com/environment/TRC.asp) claims that this solution (source reduction) is better even than recycling, as it has lower environmental impacts. For example, the website states:

> to deliver one serving of chilli (14.29oz), Tetra Recart requires 0.63oz of packaging; steel cans require 1.76oz of packaging. For every 1,000 servings, Tetra Recart requires 39lbs of packaging; steel cans require 110lbs of packaging. If we assume that 58% of steel cans are recycled, then 64lbs are recycled and 46lbs becomes trash. Therefore, even if no Tetra Recart is recycled, Tetra Recart still creates 15% less trash – 39lbs of Tetra Recart, compared to 46lbs of steel cans! Since Tetra Recart is recyclable where beverage cartons are recycled, Tetra Recart creates even less waste.

In short, if the full supply chain is considered and developed accordingly there are substantial savings possible at many levels.

Source: www.tetrapakusa.com/environment/TRC.asp; Author calculations; L Sparks (2005) Boxing clever: the shape of things to come?, *Food Manufacture*, 7 January, p 28.

CASE J: REUSABLE PLASTIC CONTAINERS, CALIFORNIA

In 1999 a field test was conducted to examine the economic, environmental and performance feasibility of shipping and displaying fresh product in supermarkets. Reusable plastic containers (RPCs) use was tested with grapes and carrots in four supermarkets in Alameda County, California. These products represent above-average products for such container use, so are to an extent a 'best case' test.

Obstacles to widespread adoption of RPCs for produce can be significant. These barriers include inertia or resistance to change, uncertainty as to the most efficient business model, and variations in how economic and suitable RPCs are for a particular product or shipping solution. This field test tried to address these questions.

The 19-week test involved four stores using RPCs exclusively for table grapes and baby carrots for the study period, together with four control stores. Weekly audits and personal interviews were used to gather data. Six major findings emerged:

1. Cost savings from using RPCs vary widely but are often significant. Labour saving by not having to unpack the container and to hand-stack the retail display and by not having to pay the cost of disposal are the main saving generators.

2. This test did not support the concern of some grocers that using RPCs for display will negatively affect sales.

3. Growers/packers in this test were neutral or supportive of RPCs.

4. Whether RPCs should be owned, leased or pooled is unclear.

5. RPCs would partially reduce the volume and waste of product containers used in the area.

6. Acceptance of RPCs by grocers increases with experience.

Conclusions

This test showed that, under these circumstances, there were sufficient potential economic, performance and environmental advantages to encourage the further use of RPCs by grocers. This would provide benefits generally but particularly in source reduction. The keys to enhanced use include:

- the generation of credible practical examples;

- the collection and sharing of information;

- the reliable supply of clean, serviceable RPCs;

- a critical mass of RPC users to establish a viable network.

Source: This case summary has been adapted from BRC (2000) *Feasibility of Reusable Plastic Containers (RPCs) for Shipping and Displaying Produce*, BRC, Menlo Park, CA, http://www.stopwaste.org/docs/ 221547412005rpces.pdf and http://www.stopwaste.org/docs/ rpcapp.pdf [accessed 10 November 2005]. This material is republished with permission from StopWaste.Org (a waste prevention and recycling public agency in Alameda County, California – see www.StopWaste.Org).

CONCLUSIONS

Ten application case studies have been presented in this chapter. These have ranged considerably in origin, scale and scope, with various issues being addressed. Table 7.5 attempts to provide a summary of key issues as seen on a case-by-case basis. Readers may take different messages and lessons from the cases, but these appear to be the significant ones from our perspective.

Five aspects of the cases and lessons can be drawn out, as they appear to reflect overarching themes:

1. There is clearly an issue over the *approach* to be adopted. The cases illustrate both a dominant designer and a more collaborative approach. In some cases the collaboration is a partnership between two major players, but in others it is system-wide. The choice of approach and of partners and the implications for those organizations omitted from initial developments can be significant. The significance arises in terms of issues around speed of development, costs of adjustment and investment, and proliferation of sizes and shapes.

2. Many of the cases show a variety of benefits from consideration of packaging logistics, which suggests that a second overarching point is the *scope* of the possibilities. Some of the cases demonstrate essentially highly detailed and apparently small changes that turn out to have real significance. Others are about system-wide standardization with implications across many supply chain organizations and in many directions.

3. The cases also point to a variety of *operational* changes consequent on alterations to packaging logistics. Many of the cases raise issues about how to accommodate changed practices and behaviours. The 'problem' in a supply chain perspective is of course that the interconnections amongst components of the supply chain point to widespread operational consequences. Whether it is a small change in design or the development of a whole new system, operational consequences are considerable. In order to have viable systems, there needs to be operational effort expended in structuring and scaling the system requirements.

4. Many of the cases contain some aspect of *consumer* acceptance or otherwise. Whilst customer acceptance in the supply chain is one

Table 7.5 Application case studies – lessons

Title of Case	Lessons
A Kisten-Pool, Austria	Market-driven adoption due to benefits. Non-profit association model. Quality benefits for consumers. Need for standardization and agreement.
B Versfust Project, Netherlands	Modular approach by company and crate manufacturer. Interstackability, modularity and standardization. Specifications presented to market (dominant design). Conversion problems. Issues of returns and cleansing.
C Tine Milk, Norway	Roll-rack cage developed to reduce handling and improve flow. Shelf-ready display. Interstackability of empty roll-rack cages. Limited system-wide acceptance and use due to standardization.
D Packaging development in FMCG, Sweden	Shelf-ready merchandising test unit developed. Handling time decreased and sales increased. Manufacturers needed to invest. Problems over smaller pallet sizes. Some residual handling issues. Trade-offs between logistics efficiency and consumer acceptance.
E Packaging and display, Sweden	Display units of different forms tested. Standardization affects operations. Trade-offs between handling and consumer accessibility. Packaging affects positioning and segment value, as well as supply systems operations.
F Fresh fruit salad packaging for airfreight, South Africa and UK	Space utilization in airfreight is a significant activity. Packaging design contributes to product quality and logistics costs.
G Packaging for air cargo, South Africa and UK	Speed in air cargo delivery can be critical. Temperature regimes affect the products and need to be controlled. Critical hazard points need monitoring. Logistics packaging reduces risks if undertaken correctly.
H Mercadona, Spain	Shelf-ready merchandising systems aid retailing. Presentation via logistics can be strongly positive. Traceability of equipment and product a developing area, with RFID an option.
I Sainsbury – from cans to cartons, UK	Small packaging changes can have large implications for logistics. Weight and volume are key considerations in logistics, but shape is also significant. Consumer reactions need monitoring.
J Reusable plastic containers, California	Testing reusable containers showed large benefits. Obstacles remain to system-wide acceptance. Consumer acceptance in store was good. Viable widespread network needed.

issue, consumer acceptance at the retail store remains critical. A number of the cases point to the trade-off that is required/ necessitated between the principles of logistics efficiency and the visual selling function of products and packaging in the store. Logistics solutions that do not encourage consumer purchase may not be the most sustainable or sensible way forward. It is in these areas of consumer acceptance, merchandising and in-store selling that corrugated packaging may have advantages.

5. Finally, the issue of scale of packaging logistics systems and reusable or returnable systems raises the issue of *traceability* of the basic equipment and product. Implied in many of the cases (and indeed throughout this book) is a move from disposable to returnable systems of packaging. In such a case there is a need to track the returnable system components. With particular emphasis in fresh food, there are also dimensions of product traceability and hazard analysis to be considered. As indicated in some of the cases, technological developments may be possible to assist in this area (discussed further in Chapter 9).

These overarching themes are important in their own right and build upon the issues discussed earlier in the book. They also, however, raise another aspect of the subject, namely how organizations and managers choose between these competing considerations and pressures and how they consider the implications of their choices and options. Chapter 8 attempts to assist in this process of choice.

8 Change Drivers in Packaging Logistics

It is now appropriate to attempt to make a more comprehensive review of the way in which the key drivers of change can work together to bring about varying degrees of success in the implementation of packaging logistics for fresh food retailing. This chapter builds on the descriptive and theoretical basis of the earlier chapters of the book and incorporates the main elements of the practical lessons derived from the contrasting case study models described in Chapter 6 as well as the array of more specific application case studies from Chapter 7. The intention is to develop, using these foundations, an integrated or holistic view of the distinctive components central to this book, retailing logistics, fresh food packaging, and the challenge of change management. The intention in this chapter is to provide the practical operator with a checklist of items that will be needed for evaluation in their consideration of the scope for change in their supply chains.

There are many drivers and enablers of change. We have covered many of these in the earlier chapters on food retailing (Chapter 2), retail logistics (Chapter 3), packaging (Chapter 4) and change management (Chapter 5). Those chapters also identified some of the barriers preventing the success of the full implementation of packaging logistics change. These barriers provide some of the explanation as to why some companies cannot accomplish the improvements that they strive to achieve. Not only do these barriers need to be identified in practice as part of any evaluation process but there also needs to be a method of resolving any difficulties identified so as to achieve appropriate solutions. A key aim of this chapter is to provide insights that can help identify those barriers and change catalysts in considering packaging logistics solutions in fresh food retailing. This process should help identify ways to achieve a more efficient and cost-effective handling and distribution for fresh foods in both domestic and global supply systems.

The structure of this chapter is deliberately designed to attempt to help practising operators assess the position of their own operation in this interaction of retail change, organization change and packaging change. This chapter should help operators reflect on the status of their own organization and its supply chain. This can be achieved by a process of self-assessment of the opportunities and barriers that are encountered while undertaking the task of implementing change in the field of packaging logistics.

The integrated or holistic view is presented here through the reconsideration of our original diagram of three overlapping circles representing retail change, packaging change and logistics change (see Figure 8.1). The interaction amongst and between the topics is symbolized by an area of overlap. The topics themselves have been introduced in earlier chapters and the interactions examined primarily through the use of major and application case studies. The zones of integration and overlap are identified in Figure 8.1 by letters:

A – retail and logistics change;

B – packaging and retail change;

C – supply chain (logistics and packaging) change;

D – managing packaging logistics change.

For each of these zones, it is possible to create lists, A, B, C and D, of their active drivers, critical success factors, barriers and solutions. These can then be used in the evaluation process by individual organizations. The preparation for and application of the evaluation process is outlined in Figure 8.2. Each of the four lists (see Figure 8.2) provides sufficient structure for an operator to conduct an evaluation and identify the level of achievement of a company and its fresh food supply chain. These

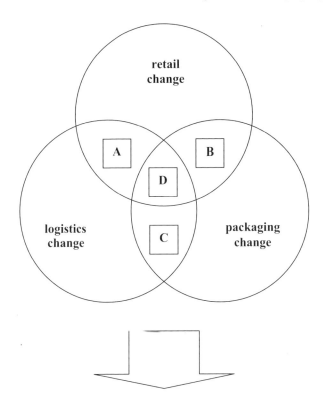

Figure 8.1   *Packaging, logistics, retailing and supply chain organization change management*

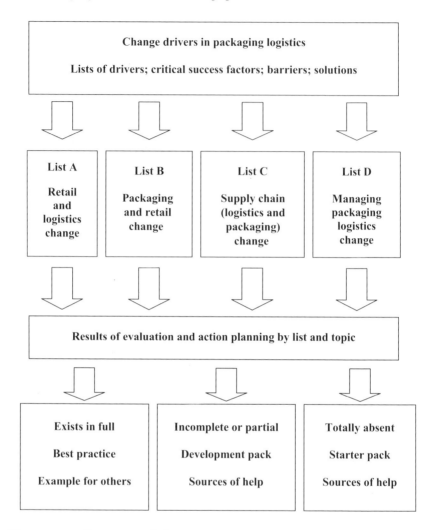

Figure 8.2   *Structure of the process outlined in this chapter*

levels could, for example, show best practice for a company in need of development or even as a new entrant in this field. From undertaking this evaluation process, an organization should develop enough data to construct either a development pack or a starter pack according to the needs of the situation and thus to address the identified needs.

THE EVALUATION AND ACTION PLANNING PROCESS

Before examining the lists in more detail, it is worth describing a possible evaluation method that an operator may wish to use. There are several steps in this evaluation process (see Figure 8.3), and this process needs to

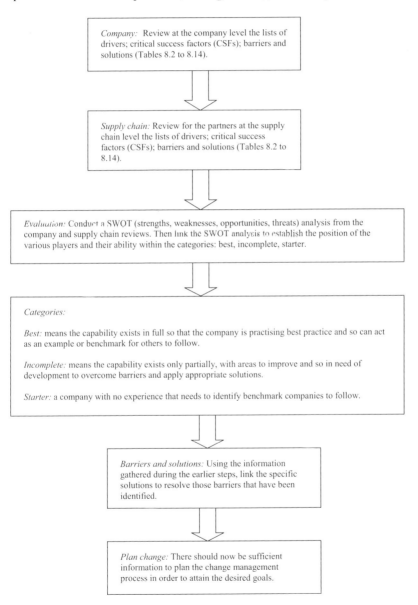

Figure 8.3   *Steps in the evaluation and action process*

be undertaken both generally and for specific sub-areas of packaging or supply chain activities. The starting point is to conduct an internal review at company level and identify its strengths and weaknesses, and so concentrate on where further development is required. The next step is to look at the partners up and down the fresh food supply chain and evaluate their capacity for managing packaging logistics change. With this information it is possible to clarify the strengths and weaknesses of the company and its supply chain partners in the context of the opportunities and threats in this specific business environment. The categories of assessment are: 1) best or exists in full; 2) incomplete or partial; and 3) totally absent or starter. These levels become the basis for best practice, the development toolbox and the starter toolbox respectively. Companies demonstrating best practice principles can become the benchmark and example for others to follow. The development pack toolbox is more appropriate for the incomplete or partial level and will lead on to identifying the barriers to progress and acquiring the knowledge of how to improve and apply solutions to overcome these obstacles. The starter pack toolbox is appropriate for the totally absent or starter level and provides advice on how to begin. This will involve obtaining an understanding of the full range of drivers and critical success factors and how to overcome the most common obstacles and avoid the major pitfalls. The last two steps in the evaluation and action planning process are to use all this information to identify any barriers that exist and learn how to apply the specific solutions to overcome them and so move towards a successful result. The final task is to create a change management plan that will provide the critical success factors for the implementation. This will strengthen the planning and implementation stages of any change programme needed for packaging logistics and fresh food retailing.

LISTS OF DRIVERS, CRITICAL SUCCESS FACTORS, BARRIERS AND SOLUTIONS

Now that we have described the broad evaluation and action planning process, it is appropriate to move on to the lists of drivers, critical success factors, barriers and solutions. We have provided broad structures here. The general approach is presented in Figure 8.3 and Table 8.1. The detailed supporting lists can be found in Tables 8.2 to 8.14 in the Appendix at the end of this chapter. There are four main lists that summarize the earlier research, theory and case studies. These four categories are:

A – retail change relating to the fresh food supply chain;

B – packaging change relating to fresh food retail logistics;

C – change relating to the supply chain and packaging; and

D – managing packaging logistics change.

Tables 8.2 to 8.14 found in the Appendix at the end of this chapter provide detailed information. They are there to be used by those who wish to conduct evaluations about packaging for a company and its fresh food supply chain. Their content reflects the specific focus of this book, which is on packaging logistics for fresh food retailing. There are many other considerations from management or specialist perspectives that are not included here since they would be outside the scope of the book. In other words, whilst the structure and information provided here in these lists and tables are a way into the evaluation, companies need to be aware of specific situations and circumstances as they pertain to them. The tables and lists are indicative rather than exhaustive in that regard.

List A: Retail change relating to the fresh food supply chain (Tables 8.2 to 8.4)

There are three strong influences that shape the fresh food supply chain in today's retailing business: daily demand for fresh food, the need for the 'right' freshness, and retail leadership and pace in the supply chain. Customers are demanding a daily supply of fresh product throughout the year, and retailing and fresh food supply chains need to be structured and organized to supply this daily demand for fresh product. Part of this structure is a logistics organization that can deliver fresh product to the retail outlets 'at the right freshness' so that it is in a condition that is correct for the product and provides the customer with as long a shelf-life in the home as is possible. This is a critical success factor for the mass sale of fresh products. It is part of delivering the marketing promise. The final and highly significant influence on the fresh food supply chain is the leadership from retailers. They set the pace of fresh food logistics and take on the responsibility of leadership and supply chain direction with most suppliers. There may well be situations where the retailers have yet to take on this role but that is only a matter of time given the need to meet consumer demands. Forward-looking suppliers can readily get involved in such processes by working with retailers.

List B: Packaging change relating to fresh food retail logistics (Tables 8.5 to 8.8)

The influences on packaging change relating to fresh food retail logistics flow out of the characteristics described in list A. The daily supply of fresh product requires that it is moved very rapidly along the supply chain from supplier to retail store. This has placed new handling requirements on packaging to ensure it protects the product while it is sorted, assembled and transported at speed. The movement is so fast that the leaders in the field aim not to hold stock in their distribution centres. This has implications for warehouse and distribution centre design, with a need for large floor areas in which to work and very little multiple pallet racked height. Movement, not storage, has become the key. But the most critical aspect of packaging is that it is efficient in maintaining temperature control so that the fresh product does not deteriorate no matter how extreme the ambient conditions may be. This is especially true if it is necessary for long-haul air cargo journeys between continents. The operator advice is to spend money on the proper quality of packaging in order to maximize the market value of the product when it reaches the consumer. From an environmental perspective, packaging solutions today need to be reusable and recyclable. Where this is not the case then companies need to look at those companies that are carrying out best practice and use them as a benchmark and example to follow. Finally, the research shows that packaging design depends on the vision of the function that has assumed control. Technological improvement is a highly specialist area. However, the question about how an operation should take place in the future is the responsibility of all those who understand the different parts of the activity in its new form along the supply chain. It takes a special relationship between the operator and the technical expert to forge an effective new design. This requires continually asking the technological experts to keep looking for the right type of solution for desired future applications. For others it is easier to follow an established operator that is already performing best practice, but they will always be behind best practice to some degree.

List C: Change relating to the supply chain and packaging (Tables 8.9 to 8.11)

There has been a great value in applying some of the lessons of change management to implementing change in fresh product logistics packaging. Aside from the normal management guidance about the most effective way of creating change in an organization, the key question for any supply chain is whether the companies that participate, and the supply chain itself, behave in a way that integrates or segments the players, the departments and those who should be cooperating as partners. This issue can influence the speed of implementation, its quality and the length of time taken from concept to completion. One factor that has been demonstrated to speed up implementation in packaging is the presence of a dominant player or dominant designer that takes leadership and has influence with the many stakeholders that could otherwise become blockers and barriers. For suppliers, the danger comes in situations where there are competing standards in the channel and no single solution is emerging. Additional systems add additional costs and complicate the supply chain. However, in many cases the lack of a single solution should not detract from searching for one, as otherwise stagnation and cost increases are the outcomes.

List D: Managing packaging logistics change (organizational change) (Tables 8.12 to 8.14)

Making changes in packaging logistics, especially for fresh products, can be a huge challenge. There is a great deal of labour applied in retail stores to moving fresh product from delivery vehicle to retail shelf. Retailers are always keen to work more effectively, and this is an area where it is possible to work differently and so use less resource. Retail distribution centres have a critical role in the fresh food supply chain, as they assemble orders for stores. In a high-volume, fast-moving distribution centre, there is a requirement to protect the product at the same time as this very rapid handling of goods. Packaging design has an impact on both. Research has shown that the outputs from packaging design are strongly influenced by the location of that design control point. It is critical that packaging designers visit along the whole length of the supply chain, particularly the distribution centres and the back-room operations in retailing, as experience shows that their operations are not always understood by suppliers, designers or marketing people. When the entire supply chain is considered, solutions that allow 'flow' along more of the channel may well reveal themselves.

CONCLUSIONS

The application of the evaluation and action planning process is intended to benefit those companies that wish to review and improve their fresh food supply chain and the packaging logistics aspects that assist retailers to deliver on their company's marketing promise to customers. It is indicative rather than exhaustive, but should lead to interesting questions being posed in an organization and along its supply chains. The process is in essence the summary of the lessons of the discussion and the case studies developed in this book. It details the critical areas for consideration and focus and in this way points to the centrality of appropriate packaging logistics developments to enhance supply chain functionality and effectiveness.

APPENDIX: EVALUATION AND ACTION PLANNING TABLES

Table 8.1   Lists of drivers, critical success factors, barriers and solutions

List A: Retail change relating to the fresh food supply chain
A1   Supply of daily demand for fresh product (Table 8.2).
A2   Logistics 'at the right freshness' (Table 8.3).
A3   Retailers set the pace in logistics (Table 8.4).

List B: Packaging change relating to fresh food retail logistics
B1   Rapid handling along the supply chain from supplier to retail store (Table 8.5).
B2   Efficient temperature controlled packaging (Table 8.6).
B3   Reusable packaging solutions (Table 8.7).
B4   Packaging design control point (Table 8.8).

List C: Change relating to the supply chain and packaging
C1   Identification of companies and supply chains as integrated or segmentalist (Table 8.9).
C2   Fast or slow pace of implementation and timescales (Table 8.10).
C3   Role of the dominant player or dominant designer in leadership (Table 8.11).

List D: Managing packaging logistics change
D1   Incorporating the needs of retail at the store to move fresh food products (Table 8.12).
D2   Attending to the needs of retail distribution centres to handle fresh food products (Table 8.13).
D3   Where to stand when designing packaging logistics for fresh food retailing (Table 8.14).

Table 8.2　List A: Retail change relating to the fresh food supply chain – List A1: Supply of daily demand for fresh product

What success looks like: the retailer can successfully source fresh product for its customers for daily purchase from home and around the world.

1	*Drivers and critical success factors*
1a	Consumers want fresh products.
1b	Use of consumer demand data from electronic point of sale (EPOS).
1c	Information technology and rapid data flow along the supply chain.
1d	Preparation of fresh products for display, eg flowers, vegetables, fresh meat.
2	*Barriers to success*
2a	Data flow incomplete, disjointed or not fast enough for daily action.
2b	Suppliers not fully part of the process and lacking in responsiveness.
2c	Logistics infrastructure not in place.
2d	Product not available for daily purchase by consumers.
3	*Solutions to overcome barriers*
3a	Implement a comprehensive supply data strategy including web-based options.
3b	Work with suppliers to bring them on board with the strategy.
3c	Logistics can be subcontracted to experienced professional companies.
3d	Find alternative sources of product to match supply seasons with retail demand.

Table 8.3　List A: Retail change relating to the fresh food supply chain – List A2: Logistics 'at the right freshness'

What success looks like: all parties in the temperature controlled supply chain operate with strict control and so deliver fresh products in peak condition for consumers.

1	*Drivers and critical success factors*
1a	Food safety legislation standards.
1b	Need for complete integrity throughout the chill chain.
1c	Global and local sourcing of fresh products as appropriate.
1d	Use of air cargo for international movements of fresh products where appropriate.
2	*Barriers to success*
2a	Chill chain disciplines lacking and so exposing the product to wrong temperatures.
2b	Transport and warehousing not properly temperature controlled.
2c	Exposure when product is moved or in transit between vehicle, warehouses and retail.
2d	Organization not in place among all members along the whole supply chain.
3	*Solutions to overcome barriers*
3a	Education of all channel staff on detrimental effects of poor discipline on product quality.
3b	Benchmark standards in transport and warehousing on successful companies.
3c	Conduct hazard risk analysis on the whole supply chain and implement controls.
3d	Identify problem areas with specific members and promote control between them.

Table 8.4   List A: Retail change relating to the fresh food supply chain – List A3: Retailers set the pace in logistics

What success looks like: the retailer is in a commanding position with extensive, even global, control and reach and can create an administrative vertical integration of the supply chain.

1	*Drivers and critical success factors*
1a	Increase in scale of retail organizations.
1b	Strength of retail branding.
1c	Concentration and use of retail power to meet consumer demands.
1d	Retail internationalization of sourcing and retail operations.

2	*Barriers to success*
2a	No leadership within the supply chain.
2b	Fragmented components or players in the value chain.
2c	Suppliers using a 'push' method of deciding what to send out of their production.
2d	The pace required by consumers not being achieved by the whole supply chain.

3	*Solutions to overcome barriers*
3a	Raise the issues to board level and obtain top-level backing.
3b	Transform the supply chain into an integrated group of partners.
3c	Change to a 'pull' method of determining quantities and products for consumers.
3d	Set up workshops with partners to sort out how to achieve the correct pace.

Table 8.5   List B: Packaging change relating to fresh food retail logistics – List B1: Rapid handling along the supply chain from supplier to retail store

What success looks like: the whole fresh product supply chain is operating at a high throughput and short transit time from the supplier to the consumer at the retail store for both domestic and global sourcing.

1	*Drivers and critical success factors*
1a	Zero stock holding in the supply chain.
1b	Interstackability of fresh products from different suppliers.
1c	Traceability of product through the supply chain route back to the supplier.

2	*Barriers to success*
2a	Lack of product availability or timing mismatch of supply and order.
2b	Lack of the right kind of capacity in logistics for movement not storage.
2c	The organization not being set up for this rapid pace of action.
2d	Inappropriate methods of handling that are neither interstackable nor fast.

3	*Solutions to overcome barriers*
3a	Multifunctional review of supply and order processes and timing.
3b	Learn from successful benchmark companies and how they have changed.
3c	Examine root causes of the problem and set up workshops with partners.
3d	Set up the required traceability controls from supplier to retailer.

Table 8.6   List B: Packaging change relating to fresh food retail logistics – List B2: Efficient temperature controlled packaging

What success looks like: all parties, and in particular suppliers, understand and implement the correct level of packaging protection for temperature controlled movements.

1   Drivers and critical success factors
1a   Packaging strength and security in moist, humid or wet conditions.
1b   Breathability of packaging for fresh fruit, vegetables, flowers.
1c   Product temperature protection during journey transitions.
1d   Insulation to preserve temperature control during the extremes of transport, eg airfreight.

2   Barriers to success
2a   Damp or moisture penetrating packaging, resulting in a collapse of wet packages.
2b   Absence of breathability perforations and release of gases during transport.
2c   Poor thermal insulation materials and methods.
2d   Lack of knowledge that transport may require a high specification of insulation material and proper methods of wrapping and handling products, eg air cargo.

3   Solutions to overcome barriers
3a   Obtain technical advice about moisture conditions during transportation.
3b   Obtain technical advice about breathability requirements and solutions.
3c   Invest in proper thermal insulation to protect the value of the product.
3d   Obtain information and advice from successful transport operators.

Table 8.7   List B: Packaging change relating to fresh food retail logistics – List B3: Reusable packaging solutions

What success looks like: all parties understand and implement reusable packaging solutions for fresh products that meet the requirements of waste and recycling legislation.

1   Drivers and critical success factors
1a   Waste and recycling legislation.
1b   Options using corrugated or plastic.
1c   Solutions fit store merchandising and consumer requirements.

2   Barriers to success
2a   One-trip packaging design.
2b   Absence of recovery or recycling infrastructure.
2c   Many incompatible designs that do not nest or interstack with each other.
2d   Resistance from suppliers or retailers to changes, eg plastic trays.

3   Solutions to overcome barriers
3a   Examine reusable packaging of successful benchmark companies.
3b   Consider the option of contracting out recovery and recycling.
3c   Rationalize and simplify the range of design, using successful benchmark companies.
3d   Hold workshops with relevant parties and successful benchmark companies.

Table 8.8   List B: Packaging change relating to fresh food retail logistics – List B4: Packaging design control point

What success looks like: the initiating party is also the packaging design control point and is aware of the technological developments. As a strong leader, it can adopt a strategy of stipulating the functionality and getting technology developed to find the solution.

1   *Drivers and critical success factors*
1a   Awareness of technological developments and change.
1b   Strategy of stipulating functionality now and for the future and sourcing technological developments to find the solution, eg the use of bale arms for the empty nesting of plastic crates.
1c   Development of retail-ready packaging/shelf-ready merchandising.

2   *Barriers to success*
2a   Ignorance of technological developments or potential future changes.
2b   Not having the status or power to influence the packaging supply companies.
2c   Trying to apply solutions piecemeal without taking on the whole system.
2d   Focusing on a range of ideas, not the most necessary solutions.

3   *Solutions to overcome barriers*
3a   Examine packaging technology solutions of successful benchmark companies.
3b   Open contact with key suppliers of packaging and their development departments.
3c   Make an assessment of the total system required first, and then apply the components.

Table 8.9   List C: Change relating to the supply chain and packaging – List C1: Identification of companies and supply chains as integrated or segmentalist

What success looks like: the company and its partners in the supply chain are (and act as) an integrated team to achieve outstanding results.

1   *Drivers and critical success factors*
1a   Collaboration with or without strong leadership.

2   *Barriers to success*
2a   The presence of segmentalist companies as partners in the supply chain.
2b   The supply chain itself behaving in a segmentalist manner.
2c   Incomplete vision of the supply chain.
2d   Silo management culture and fragmented effort.

3   *Solutions to overcome barriers*
3a   Obtain senior board backing for a change to an integrated company culture.
3b   Bring together the more influential players in the supply chain to assist change.
3c   Provide a comprehensive structure of the full length of the supply chain.
3d   Engage in some inter-company cultural exchange at senior level.

Table 8.10   List C: Change relating to the supply chain and packaging
– List C2: Fast or slow pace of implementation and timescales

What success looks like: the pace of implementation is swift and effective and
the change management has a senior mandate from the board for its
implementation goals.

1   Drivers and critical success factors
1a   Presence of senior, eg board-level, mandate for implementation goals.
1b   Multidisciplinary teams.
1c   Looking to future needs not current issues.

2   Barriers to success
2a   Level of influence within the company too junior.
2b   Participation from one or only a few of the relevant functions.
2c   Being bogged down in current minutiae.

3   Solutions to overcome barriers
3a   Obtain senior board backing for the implementation strategy.
3b   Bring together the full range of multidisciplinary members so a full
      view is obtained.

Table 8.11   List C: Change relating to the supply chain and packaging
– List C3: Role of the dominant player or dominant designer in
leadership

What success looks like: the change management is led by a dominant player or
dominant designer.

1   Drivers and critical success factors
1a   Presence of a dominant player in the supply chain.
1b   Presence of a dominant designer in the packaging solution.
1c   All the parties in the supply chain work together with the leader interactively.

2   Barriers to success
2a   The absence of a dominant player or dominant designer.
2b   The parties in the supply chain not working interactively with the leader.
2c   The leader not taking an integrated view of the objectives.
2d   Power struggle between large companies, eg between retailer and supplier.

3   Solutions to overcome barriers
3a   Raise the problem to the top of the most influential companies to find a
      solution.
3b   Bring together the influential players in the supply chain to promote
      interaction.
3c   Increase the involvement of the other players with the leader so they are
      accepted.
3d   The trend is to increasing power by the retailer so shift the balance to retail.

Table 8.12   List D: Managing packaging logistics change – List D1: Incorporating the needs of retail at the store to move fresh food products

What success looks like: packaging logistics design attends also to the needs of retail store handling from the delivery vehicle to the shelf for the consumer.

1   *Drivers and critical success factors*
1a   Efficiency of unloading the delivery vehicle at the retail back door to filling the retail shelf.
1b   Making fresh products available for consumers swiftly.
1c   Retail need to do this with the minimum retail labour cost, eg one-touch refill, shelf-ready merchandising.

2   *Barriers to success*
2a   Supplier-only perspective.
2b   Marketing-only perspective.
2c   No or limited knowledge of retail operations.

3   *Solutions to overcome barriers*
3a   Create workshop or video evidence about the needs of the retail store operation.
3b   Create workshop or video evidence about the labour resource in the retail store.
3c   Create an interdisciplinary seminar in a retail store with other parties.

Table 8.13   List D: Managing packaging logistics change – List D2: Attending to the needs of retail distribution centres to handle fresh food products

What success looks like: packaging logistics solutions include the needs of retail distribution centres to handle fresh products, especially the matter of the interstackability of products from different suppliers.

1   *Drivers and critical success factors*
1a   Fresh food products from different suppliers have to be stacked – 'interstackability'.

2   *Barriers to success*
2a   Omission of distribution handling requirements.
2b   Power balance not recognizing the importance of distribution.
2c   The packaging designs preventing interstackability and the product being damaged.

3   *Solutions to overcome barriers*
3a   Create workshop or video evidence of the distribution operations.
3b   Set up a multidisciplinary seminar in a distribution centre for other parties.
3c   Provide visual or hands-on evidence of the benefits of good interstackability.

Table 8.14 List D: Managing packaging logistics change – List D3: Where to stand when designing packaging logistics for fresh food retailing

What success looks like: the design point needs to include the logistics of the supply chain and have sufficient power to influence all the parties in the value chain.

1   Drivers and critical success factors
1a   The design point includes the logistics of the entire supply chain.
1b   The 'right place to stand' has sufficient power to influence all parties.

2   Barriers to success
2a   The designer standing in only one part, with no knowledge of the whole operation.
2b   There not being sufficient influence to bring about change.
2c   The influential parties in the value chain not being included in the change process.
2d   Key stakeholders not giving their support.

3   Solutions to overcome barriers
3a   Create a multidisciplinary seminar in the critical place with all parties.
3b   Raise the issue to board level to influence or to persuade the other parties.
3c   Create inter-company workshops so all parts of the supply chain are involved.
3d   Identify key stakeholders early in the process and find ways of gaining their support.

9   *Conclusions*

This book has been designed to encourage both practitioners and academics to examine the subject of packaging logistics, both generally and in particular with respect to fresh food supply and retailing. It should be clear that, whilst the developments in fresh food are of interest, packaging logistics applies elsewhere in other supply chains as well. We hope to encourage all businesses to consider how and where some of the principles used in this book can be applied. Here, we have only scratched the surface of the possibilities.

We are also aware that we have couched this exploration in terms mainly of returnable or plastic packaging. We are firm believers that both plastic and paper packaging have key roles to play in the retail supply chain. They each have merits and have applications in both different and similar circumstances (eg Twede and Clarke, 2004). Whilst our emphasis has been on the use of returnable and plastic packaging, many of the same principles also apply in the packaging world in general. However, we would argue that many of the benefits of using returnable systems are so significant that their use will continue to increase in retail supply chains.

PACKAGING LOGISTICS IN FRESH FOOD RETAILING

This book has tried to emphasize a number of key points about the fresh food supply chain. In doing this, it has taken an avowedly supply chain and integrationist stance. This is necessary, as the pressures on retailing, particularly in the supply of fresh food, are quite extreme. If integration and cooperation and coordination do not exist in the retail supply chain for fresh food, then costs will escalate, availability for consumers is likely to be reduced and overall service levels will not be appropriate for the markets served.

The changes in retailing have been considerable in terms of the scale and location of retail stores and the product ranges that have been developed. Retailers have become increasingly concerned to control and manage the supply chain of fresh food products (and others) in order to meet these consumer demands. Information movement has increasingly replaced physical product movement. One implication of this has been the increasing concern to move products at appropriate times, to the correct locations, and often with very limited lead times or time delivery windows. As a consequence, issues of ease of flow and reducing time spent in handling (including on packaging) have come to the fore. Additionally, environmental concerns about the overuse of packaging in handling systems have added to cost pressures to reconsider packaging ideas in logistics systems.

This book has considered the issues around this emerging topic of packaging logistics. To allow manageability of the topic it has focused on fresh food logistics (though similar principles can be used in other product sectors – see the case on IKEA by Gustafsson *et al*, 2005). The core of the book has been two major case studies, together with the selection of 10 smaller application case studies, drawn from a variety of situations, perspectives and countries. These have been considered within a framework of retail, logistics and packaging change. Given the widespread implications of changing aspects of packaging logistics, the notion of managing or directing change has been a key component of the book and of the major cases.

This book has been written with two perspectives in mind: an academic one and a practitioner one. From an academic perspective, the main elements have been discussed as the book progressed. Essentially they focus on the complex issues of organizing modern fresh food retail logistics and how this fits with conceptual and theoretical models of supply chain management and behaviour. From a practitioner perspective, Chapter 8 has been devised and designed to encourage operational reflection on the position within particular supply chains. It is hoped that this provides a set of mechanisms to encourage improvement in supply chains wherever they are found.

This book thus contains a number of key messages for different audiences. Two overarching comments, however, need to be made. First, the importance of packaging logistics has been, but cannot continue to be, overlooked by many supply chain organizations. The significance of developments outlined here in cost and service terms demands that packaging logistics be taken seriously. Secondly, there is no such thing as a fixed supply chain system in the sense that current demands and development in the future (see below) will undoubtedly create new possibilities and practices in supply chains across the globe. Standing still in modern supply chain management and packaging logistics is not a sustainable future option.

FUTURE PERSPECTIVES

There are many issues and lessons already discussed that will continue to have an impact in the future. As supply chains continue to be refined, so the issues of change management in packaging logistics will continue to concern many businesses. There are, however, also a number of other issues, some of which have been touched on in this book, that are likely to play a key role in this area in the future. A brief consideration of some of these would appear to be an appropriate way to conclude this book. Table 9.1 provides some of the details. Full discussion of all of these areas in depth is not possible here, but some comments on each area are needed.

Global or international supply systems

For many retailers, the act of retailing is no longer a local or a national affair. The largest food retailers in the world have extensive international supply and retailing operations. This appears likely to continue as a trend in coming years. There are a number of dimensions to this. First, there has been a transference of sourcing from home markets to lower-cost markets generally. As a result, many retailers have a very wide range of countries from which they source. Secondly, there is some concentration within this network of countries, particularly on the large and emerging market in China. Thus, in 2005 Wal-Mart spent $22 billion with c 20,000 suppliers in China. Metro, the German

Table 9.1   Issues for the future

Global or International Supply Systems	These are already here in many industries, but there is likely to be a further expansion in the scope and reach of such systems.
Local and Home Supply Systems	At the other extreme, there is increasing interest in tailored local solutions and home delivery systems, adding complexity.
Shelf-Ready Packaging and Merchandising Units	The use of flow-through systems has encouraged the placing of merchandise directly on the shop floor and shelves. There is a tension here between appropriate logistics systems and systems for selling products. Shelf-ready packaging allows one-touch replenishment on to existing shelves.
RFiD	As the cost of RfID chips falls, so their potential for tracking packaging solutions (through embedded identity), as well as products, rises.

retailer, notes that 64 per cent of its supplies on its global procurement list are from China. There are thus issues of scale and breadth in sourcing to be considered.

The range of countries used by retailers obviously complicates the supply chain position. There need to be duplicative systems and investment and learning by suppliers and infrastructure development to allow cost-effective sourcing. On the other hand, however, there has to be some concern about putting so much investment into one country – China – which must at some point reach capacity levels, let alone other concerns about its future expansion, eg trade quotas. There are difficult choices for retailers to make.

There are of course further logistical implications of international sourcing. There are changed trade-offs in terms of packaging weight and cost, depending on the transportation mechanisms used. The cost of labour, capital and equipment varies across these countries, producing optimal, but different, country solutions. As suppliers and countries start from different positions, so there is a danger of differently standardized solutions emerging, yet the costs of implementing a fully standardized, or 'Western', solution may be high. Again, the decision matrix outlined earlier is complicated by the emerging

sourcing realities on a global stage. That is why this book has information and even lessons that are applicable to retailers and suppliers
across the globe.

Local and home supply systems

In contrast to the globalization and internationalization of supply
chains discussed above, many food retailers have become increasingly
interested in aspects of store embeddedness in the local community.
The definition of 'local' appears to vary by product and situation, but a
number of aspects of localness or locality come to the fore. First is the
concern to tailor the store product range to local tastes and preferences
by accommodating local products and local producers. Secondly, the
advent of technology has been used to provide home delivery in local
areas for grocery products, thus 'tying in' consumers to stores. Both
have considerable packaging and general logistics implications.

In the first case, there are a number of solutions to the 'local product'
issues. Some involve branding and labelling and are not truly of
concern here. More importantly, the question of how small local
suppliers can provide their products into large-scale distribution units
has been taxing retailers and suppliers. As systems become more standardized and centralized so the opportunities (and costs) to deliver
small-scale loads in small areas (even a single store) become more
difficult to realize. Retailers want such linkages, as their consumers are
wanting the product, but quite how the producers can link to the stores
or distribution centres is often the stumbling point. Requiring standardized or specialist packaging for transport or handling can add to
the problems. This issue requires practical solutions and assistance to
local producers.

The second issue of home delivery is less contentious in that
retailers have realized that standard transport and delivery systems
can be adopted irrespective of where the picking takes place. Thus
specialist home delivery vehicles can be constructed around basic
crate/box/tray solutions (Figure 9.1). These allow an effective use of
space and provide an appropriate solution. Work remains to be done
on the packaging of items to fit better into such boxes, but the basic
shape of the process has been developed (aided by being closed-loop
operations in most situations). An interesting question is whether
consumers can be persuaded to take more ownership of the delivery
packaging solutions and even to do so in standard retail settings
(Figure 9.2). By removing plastic bags and other disposable packaging

Figure 9.1   *Home delivery systems in the UK* (source: *author photographs, 2005*)

Figure 9.1a

Figure 9.1b

Figure 9.2   *Collapsible plastic boxes for consumer purchase and use*
(source: *author photograph, 2005*)

from the point of sale and delivery (possibly even by legal steps, as in Ireland), it may be possible to persuade customers to invest in reusable facilities/equipment, with possible consequent environmental benefits. The full environmental and cost implications of such consumer-focused changes remain somewhat unclear and much debated.

Shelf-ready packaging and merchandising units

This book has emphasized the role of packaging logistics in improving the efficiency and effectiveness of supply chains. At various points, the issue of the potentially competing pressures of handling efficiencies and store merchandising acceptability have been raised. Additionally, many food retailers have come under considerable pressure to improve on-shelf availability, but not at the expense of the visual impact of the products in the store. These tensions have increased and solutions are now being sought. In some products, the solution has been to use dollies to speed up handling or to develop merchandisable units that can be 'rolled' into place. (Figure 3.2 shows this change in banana retailing/merchandising.)

The terminology in this area is still developing, and a variety of terms is being used to discuss broadly similar or related activities. The IGD and ECR UK have proposed (IGD/ECR UK, 2005) that 'shelf ready packaging' be used as a term for a product that comes ready-merchandised and that can be put directly on to a shelf. 'Retail ready packaging' is their term for additional aspects of easy identification and easy packaging opening, but where the outer case is moved direct to the shelf following 'one-touch replenishment' principles. IGD/ECR UK use the term 'display ready packaging' for stand-alone units that are 'moved into space', such as on merchandising units or soft drinks dollies. Figure 9.3 provides some examples of these approaches.

In one sense the terminology does not matter here. What is important is that the principles of packaging logistics are being followed through to the retail end of the supply chain. Table 9.2 identifies the key attributes of retail ready packaging as identified by IGD/ECR UK (2005). The trials that retailers have been undertaking have shown increased availability on-shelf and increased sales. This is combined with improved store labour efficiencies (and possible enhanced distribution facilities) and better quality of product in-store.

Such developments are the logical conclusion of many of the issues that have been discussed in this book. There are likely to be more and more such demands from retailers. Manufacturers and distributors are going to have to alter their approaches accordingly and in partnership with retailers. Such pressures are going to be felt across the sector and the globe. Again, hard decisions about the cost of (or not) altering packaging and production processes will be needed.

Retailers are already beginning to raise the pressure in this area and encourage suppliers to move in the 'right' direction. Tesco have

Figure 9.3   *Shelf-ready merchandising* (source: *author photographs, 2005*)

Figure 9.3a

Figure 9.3b

produced a 'Retail-ready packaging toolkit for commercial categories and suppliers' (cited at website http://www.aiccbox.org/meeting/presentations_f05/JwvdVeen-AICCpres2005-Handout-part2.pdf). This focuses on issues of availability and keeping shelves full and claims that the answer to the problems lies in 'more products in retail-ready

Table 9.2 The key attributes of retail ready packaging

Right Format	Optimized format (pack size and configuration) considering the product's merchandising destination, space and rate of sale.
Easy ID and Visibility	Right information clearly visible on the packaging to enable store personnel to identify the product quickly.
Easy Open	Packaging that can be easily opened at store level, but robust enough to remain intact throughout the supply chain.
Easy Rotate and Replenishment	RRP outers that can be easily rotated with the principles of 'one-touch replenishment'.
Easy Find and Shop	Consumer can easily identify the product to shop.
Easy Dispose/Return	Minimal use of cardboard or maximum use of returnable transit packaging.

Source: IGD/ECR UK (2005), p 9

packaging – boxes or display units that can be wheeled or placed straight on the shop floor or shelf without being unpacked. With the added bonus that they provide great opportunities for brand marketing on the tray packs and units themselves' (p 1). Retail ready packaging focuses on the need to ensure that retail packaging complexity is reduced by focusing on categories rather than single-product solutions, limited 'mainstream' solutions rather than lots of clever ideas, industry harmonization and the production of less complex packaging instructions for users. The key words are 'simplicity' and 'scale', both themes of this book.

RFID

Radio frequency identification (RFID) has been around for a long time and is used in a variety of situations. The difference now is that the cost, size and capabilities of such transponders, tags and readers have changed dramatically. Though not yet at the level to allow total item-level scope for RFID use, the price has come down sharply, encouraging major retailers such as Wal-Mart to begin to demand supplier compliance with tagging requirements.

An RFID system typically contains a tag or label embedded with a single-chip computer and an antenna, and a reader (much like a wireless LAN radio) that communicates with the tag (see www.rfid-journal.com for a glossary of terms). There are a number of variations of this basic system, and various alternative system structures can be devised based on function, activity, value, situation and cost (see Sparks and Wagner, 2004). Much remains to be sorted out in terms of RFID but the pressure to use such technology is mounting, not least because it enhances capabilities in terms of real-time packing of objects (products, pallets, boxes, etc).

A review of the potential for RFID adoption in returnable packaging has been produced by Logica CMG (2003/04). This, through a cost–benefit analysis and interviews with key companies, makes a case for the adoption of RFID in such systems. It also would seem that there is a potential case for RFID use on disposable packaging as well. As ever, the circumstances will dictate the outcomes, but it would appear that there is much potential. In particular, the capability in closed-loop systems to monitor packaging (eg boxes and pallets) and products tightly and associate the two would seem to be attractive (see 'Case H: Mercadona' in Chapter 7). Other solutions will be used in other circumstances. Given the proliferation of returnable packaging, embedded identity would seem to be an advantage, whether the system is closed-loop or not. IGD (2006) have pointed out the scale of the problem and the scale of solution needed. They estimate that, in the UK, there are over 1.6 million roll cages and 25.8 million plastic crates in circulation in the major food retailers. Keeping track of these and the products in them is a considerable task, but one that has potentially considerable returns. RFID may have a large market.

This is, however, only one of the potential applications or implications of RFID use in the retail supply chain. Many other possibilities exist and considerable experimentation is under way. For example, problems of temperature regime monitoring throughout the life of a product or along the supply chain may be one additional possibility with implications for packaging design and data capture as well as, more importantly, for food security and safety.

CONCLUDING REMARKS

This book has considered the potential benefits from developments in packaging logistics. It has looked in particular at fresh food retailing and logistics systems. Developments to date have been discussed and examples used to illustrate both what has been achieved and how the key decisions were made. As the concepts discussed in this book continue to be utilized in many situations and countries around the world, so concern grows about making the right decisions. This pressure to simplify and restructure supply systems is not going to go away. We hope that this book has in some way helped in the consideration of possibilities and alternatives.

The issues raised in this book do not concern only supply chain organizations such as retailers and suppliers. The topics discussed should be a focus of concern for the packaging industry as a whole, as well as for material suppliers into the packaging industry. Previously, attention has mainly focused on volume increase, but this alone is neither sustainable nor the most appropriate focus for the future. New perspectives are needed by all involved to exploit fully this potential of packaging logistics from product development to final use.

References

Arca Systems AB (2004) E-mail correspondence concerning trays in use in Europe

Bjärnemo, R, Jönson, G and Johnsson, M (2000) Packaging logistics in product development, 5th International Conference on Computer Integrated Manufacturing (ICCIM 2000), 28–30 March

Bourlakis, M and Weightman, P (2004) *Food Supply Chain Management*, Blackwell, Oxford

Bowlby R (2000) *Carried Away: The invention of modern shopping*, Faber & Faber, London

BRC (2000) *Feasibility of Reusable Plastic Containers (RPCs) for Shipping and Displaying Produce*, BRC, Menlo Park, CA, http://www.stopwaste.org/docs/221547412005rpces.pdf and http://www.stopwaste.org/docs/rpcapp.pdf [accessed 10 November 2005]

Burt, SL and Sparks, L (2002) Corporate branding, retailing and retail internationalisation, *Corporate Reputation Review*, 5, pp 194–212

Burt, SL and Sparks, L (2003) Power and competition in the UK retail grocery market, *British Journal of Management*, 14, pp 237–54

Christopher, M (1998) *Logistics and Supply Chain Management*, 2nd edn, FT/Prentice Hall, London

Christopher, M and Peck, H (2003) *Marketing Logistics*, 2nd edn, Butterworth-Heinemann, Oxford

CH Robinson Worldwide/Iowa State University (2001) *Temperature Controlled Logistics Report 2001–2002*, CH Robinson Worldwide, Eden Prairie, MN

Colla, E (2004) The outlook for European grocery retailing: competition and format development, *International Review of Retail, Distribution and Consumer Research*, 14 (1), pp 47–69

Cooper, J, Browne, M and Peters, M (1991) *European Logistics*, Blackwell, Oxford

Davies, RL (ed) (1995) *Retail Planning Policies in Western Europe*, Routledge, London

Dawson, JA (1995) Retail change in the European Community, in *Retail Planning Policies in Western Europe*, ed RL Davies, Ch 1, Routledge, London

Dawson, JA (2000) *Future Patterns of Retailing in Scotland*, Scottish Executive Central Research Unit, Edinburgh

Dawson, JA and Burt, SL (1998) European retailing: dynamics, restructuring and development issues, in *The New Europe: Economy, society and environment*, ed D Pinder, Ch 9, Wiley, Chichester

Dawson, JA and Lee, JH (2004) *International Retailing Plans and Strategies in Asia*, IBP, Binghamton

Dawson, JA and Shaw, SA (1990) The changing character of retailer–supplier relationships, in *Retail Distribution Management*, ed J Fernie, pp 19–39, Kogan Page, London

Dawson, JA *et al* (2003) *The Internationalisation of Retailing in Asia*, Routledge Curzon, London

Department of Transport (2003) *Key Performance Indicators for the Food Supply Chain*, Benchmarking Guide 78, Department of Transport, http://www.transportenergy.org.uk/downloads/BG78.pdf [accessed 20 May 2005]

DLF [Grocery Manufacturers of Sweden] (1990) *Logistiskt ledarskap* [Logistics Leadership], DLF, Stockholm

Dolan, C and Humphrey, J (2000) Governance and trade in fresh vegetables: the impact of UK supermarkets on the African horticulture industry, *Journal of Development Studies*, 37 (2), pp 147–76

Duffy, R and Fearne, A (2004) Partnerships and alliances in UK supermarket supply networks, in *Food Supply Chain Management*, ed MA Bourlakis and PWH Weightman, pp 136–52, Blackwell, Oxford

ElAmin, Ahmed (2005) Spanish retail achieves fresh fruit RFiD traceability, http://www.foodproductiondaily.com/news/ng.asp?id=59709, 29 April [accessed 24 October 2005]

Fearne, A and Hughes, D (2000) Success factors in the fresh produce supply chains, *British Food Journal*, 102, pp 760–72

FEFCO (2003) *Fresh Food under the Microscope*, www.fefco.org/fileadmin/ Fefco/images/Box/fefco.pdf [accessed 29 October 2004]

Fernie, J and Sparks, L (eds) (2004) *Logistics and Retail Management*, 2nd edn, Kogan Page, London

Fernie, J and Staines, H (2001) Towards an understanding of European grocery supply chains, *Journal of Retailing and Consumer Services*, 8, pp 29–36

Fisher, ML, Raman, A and McClelland, AS (2000) Rocket science retailing is almost here: are you ready?, *Harvard Business Review*, July–August, pp 115–24

Gorniak, C (2002) *The Meal Solutions Outlook to 2007*, Reuters Business Insight, London

Grant, DB, Lambert DM, Stock JR and Ellram LM (2006) *Fundamentals of Logistics Management*, European edn, McGraw-Hill, Maidenhead

Gustafsson, K (2005) The process of creating a nationwide pool system for transport packaging – from vision to decision, Licentiate thesis, Department of Design Sciences, Lund University, Lund, Sweden

Gustafsson, K, Jönson G, Smith D and Sparks L (2005) Packaging logistics and retailers' profitability: an IKEA case study, Paper presented at the 13th Research Conference of the European Association for Education and Research in Commercial Distribution, July, Lund University, Lund, Sweden

Guy, C (1994) *The Retail Development Process*, Routledge, London

Harrison, A and van Hoek, R (2002) *Logistics Management and Strategy*, Prentice Hall, London

Henson, S and Caswell, J (1999) Food safety regulation: an overview of contemporary issues, *Food Policy*, 24, pp 589–603

Hughes, A (2000) Retailers, knowledge and changing commodity networks: the case of the cut flower trade, *Geoforum*, 31, pp 175–90

Hughes, D (ed) (1994) *Breaking with Tradition: Building partnerships and alliances in the European food industry*, Wye College Press, Ashford

IGD (2006) *Retail Logistics 2006*, IGD, Watford

IGD/ECR UK (2005) *Retail Ready Packaging*, IGD, Watford, www.igd.com/ecr

Jahre, M and Hatteland, CJ (2004) Packages and physical distribution: implications for integration and standardisation, *International Journal of Physical Distribution and Logistics Management*, 34 (2), pp 123–39

Johnsson, M (1998) Packaging logistics – a value added approach, PhD dissertation, Lund University, Lund, Sweden

Kanter, RM (1984) *The Change Masters*, Wiley, New York

Koehorst, H, de Vries, H and Wubben, E (1999) Standardisation of crates: lessons from the Versfust (Freshcrate) project, *Supply Chain Management*, 4 (2), pp 95–101

Kotzab, H and Bjerre, M (eds) (2005) *Retailing in a SCM-Perspective*, Copenhagen Business School Press, Copenhagen

Kuznesof, S and Brennan, M (2004) Perceived risk and product safety in the food supply chain, in *Food Supply Chain Management*, ed MA Bourlakis and PWH Weightman, pp 32–48, Blackwell, Oxford

Larke, R and Causton, M (2005) *Japan: A modern retail superpower*, Palgrave Macmillan, Basingstoke

Lee, RJ, O'Neal DE, Pruett MW and Thomas H (1995) Planning for dominance: a strategic perspective on the emergence of a dominant design, *R&D Management*, **25** (1), pp 3–15

Lindblom, T and Rimstedt, A (2004) Retail integration strategies in the EU: Scandinavian grocery retailing, *International Review of Retail, Distribution and Consumer Research*, **14** (2), pp 171–97

Loader, R and Hobbs, JE (1999) Strategic response to food safety legislation, *Food Policy*, **24**, pp 685–706

Logica CMG (2003/04) *Making Waves: RfiD adoption in returnable packaging*, Logica CMG, Hoofddorp, http://www.logicacmg.com/pdf/RFID_study.pdf [accessed 11 November 2005]

Longstreth, R (1997) *City Center to Regional Mall*, MIT Press, Cambridge, MA

Longstreth, R (1999) *The Drive-In, the Supermarket and the Transformation of Commercial Space in Los Angeles 1914–1941*, MIT Press, Cambridge, MA

McKinnon, AC (1996) The development of retail logistics in the UK: a position paper, *Technology Foresight: Retail and Distribution Panel*, Heriot-Watt University, Edinburgh

McKinnon, AC and Campbell, J (1998) *Quick Response in the Frozen Food Supply Chain*, http://www.som.hw.ac.uk/logistics/salvesen.html [accessed 10 July 2002]

McKinsey (1998) *Driving Productivity and Growth in the UK Economy*, McKinsey, London

Marsden, T, Flynn, A and Harrison, M (2000) *Consuming Interests: The social provision of foods*, UCL Press, London

Marshall, DW (ed) (1995) *Food Choice and the Consumer*, Blackie, London

Marshall, D (2004) The food consumer and the supply chain, in *Food Supply Chain Management*, ed MA Bourlakis and PWH Weightman, pp 11–31, Blackwell, Oxford

Miller, D *et al* (1998*) Shopping, Place and Identity*, Routledge, London

Murcott, A (ed) (1998) *The Nation's Diet: The social science of food choice*, Longman, Harlow

Ogbonna, E and Wilkinson, B (1996) Inter-organizational power relations in the UK grocery industry, *International Review of Retail, Distribution and Consumer Research*, **6**, pp 395–414

Olsson, A and Györei, M (2002) Packaging through the value chain in the customer perspective marketing mix, *Packaging Technology and Science*, **15**, pp 231–39

Paine, FA (1981) *Fundamentals of Packaging*, Brookside Press, Leicester

Paine, FA (1990) *Packaging Design and Performance*, Pira, Surrey

Paine, FA and Paine, HY (1983) *A Handbook of Food Packaging*, 2nd edn, Blackie, Glasgow

Pira/University of Brighton (2004) *Packaging's Place in Society*, Summary report and technical annex, pira.co.uk [accessed 27 October 2004]

Saghir, M (2002) *Packaging Logistics Evaluation in the Swedish Retail Supply Chain*, Lund University, Lund, Sweden

Saghir, M (2004) A platform for packaging logistics development – a systems approach, Doctoral dissertation, Department of Design Sciences, Lund University, Lund, Sweden

Saghir, M and Jönson, G (2001) Packaging handling evaluation methods in the grocery retail industry, *Packaging Technology and Science*, 14, pp 21–29

Sarv, H and Landborn, J (2003) *Den systemiska innovationsstrategin – inom logistiken och andra systemdiscipliner* [The systemic innovation strategy – in logistics and other system disciplines], Vinnova, Stockholm

Seth, A and Randall, G (1999) *The Grocers: The rise and rise of the supermarket chains*, Kogan Page, London

Seth, A and Randall, G (2005) *Supermarket Wars: Global strategies for food retailers*, Palgrave Macmillan, Basingstoke

Smith, DLG (1998) Logistics in Tesco, in *Logistics and Retail Management*, ed J Fernie and L Sparks, pp 154–83, Kogan Page, London

Smith, DLG and Sparks, L (1993) The transformation of physical distribution in retailing: the example of Tesco plc, *International Review of Retail, Distribution and Consumer Research*, 3, pp 35–64

Smith, DLG and Sparks, L (2004) Logistics in Tesco: past, present and future, in *Logistics and Retail Management*, 2nd edn, ed J Fernie and L Sparks, pp 101–20, Kogan Page, London

Smith, JL, Davies, GJ and Bent, AJ (2001) Retail fast foods: overview of safe sandwich manufacture, *Journal of the Royal Society for the Promotion of Health*, 121 (4), pp 220–23

Sparks, L (1986) The changing structure of distribution in retail companies, *Transactions of the Institute of British Geographers*, 11, pp 147–54

Sparks, L (1995) Reciprocal retail internationalisation: the Southland Corporation. Ito-Yokado and 7-Eleven Convenience Stores, *Service Industries Journal*, 15 (4), pp 57–96

Sparks, L (1998) The retail logistics transformation, in *Logistics and Retail Management*, ed J Fernie and L Sparks, pp 1–22, Kogan Page, London

Sparks, L (2000a) Seven-Eleven Japan and the Southland Corporation: a marriage of convenience?, *International Marketing Review*, 17 (4/5), pp 401–15

Sparks, L (2000b) The rise of the large format food store, in *Flexible Working in Food Retailing*, ed C Baret, S Lehndorff and L Sparks, pp 1–11, Kogan Page, London

Sparks, L (2004) Retail logistics: changes and challenges, in *Logistics and Retail Management*, 2nd edn, ed J Fernie and L Sparks, pp 1–25, Kogan Page, London

Sparks, L (2005) Boxing clever: the shape of things to come?, *Food Manufacture*, 7 January, p 28

Sparks, L and Wagner, B (2004) Transforming technologies: retail exchanges and RfiD, in *Logistics and Retail Management*, 2nd edn, ed J Fernie and L Sparks, pp 188–208, Kogan Page, London

Stahre, F (1996) *Små returlastbärare i logistikkedjor: införande och effekter* [Small returnable containers in supply chains: introduction and effects], Licentiate thesis, Logistics and Transport Systems, Department of Management and Economics, Linköping University, Sweden

Sterns, PA, Codron, J-M and Reardon, T (2001) *Quality and Quality Assurance in the Fresh Product Sector: A case study of European retailers*, American Agricultural Economics Association Annual Meeting, Chicago, August, http://agecon.lib.umn.edu/ [accessed 11 July 2002]

Svenska Retursystem AB (2003) *Eurocrate, a Full-Scale Demonstration of Reusable Crates and Pallets*, Report to EU Life Research Fund, www.retursystem.se

Swahn, M and Söderburg, P (1992) *Lönsam logistik* [Profitable logistics], Teldok report no 75, Stockholm, Sweden

Twede, D (1992) The process of logistical packaging innovation, *Journal of Business Logistics*, 13, pp 69–94

Twede, D and Clarke, R (2004) Supply chain issues in reusable packaging, *Journal of Marketing Channels*, 12 (1), pp 7–26.

Underhill, P (1999) *Why We Buy: The science of shopping*, Orion, London

Waters, D (2003) *Logistics: An introduction to supply chain management*, Palgrave Macmillan, Basingstoke

Weatherspoon, D and Reardon, T (2003) The rise of supermarkets in Africa: implications for agrifood systems and the rural poor, *Development Policy Review*, 21, pp 1–17

West, M and Sparks, L (2004) Enterprise resource planning (ERP) systems: issues in implementation, in *Logistics and Retail Management*, 2nd edn, ed J Fernie and L Sparks, pp 209–30, Kogan Page, London

Wilson, N (1996a) The supply chains of perishable products in Northern Europe, *British Food Journal*, 98 (6), pp 9–15

Wilson, N (1996b) Supply chain management: a case study of a dedicated supply chain for bananas in the UK grocery market, *Supply Chain Management* 1 (2), pp 28–35

Index

FURTHER READING FROM KOGAN PAGE

Applied Transport Economics, 3rd edition, Stuart Cole, 2005

The Certificate of Professional Competence, 3rd edition, David Lowe, 2004

The Dictionary of Transport and Logistics, David Lowe, 2002

Global Logistics, 5th edition, Donald Waters, 2006

The Handbook of Logistics and Distribution Management, 3rd edition, Alan Rushton, Phil Croucher and Peter Baker, 2006

The LGV Learner Driver's Guide, John Miller, 2005

Logistics and Retail Management, 2nd edition, John Fernie and Leigh Sparks, 2004

Managing Passenger Logistics, Paul Fawcett, 2000

Managing Transport Operations, 3rd edition, Edmund J Gubbins, 2002

The Pocket Guide to LGV Drivers' Hours and Tachograph Law, 3rd edition, David Lowe, 2006

The Professional LGV Driver's Handbook, David Lowe, 2003

A Study Manual of Professional Competence in Road Haulage, 11th edition, David Lowe, 2004

The Transport Manager's and Operator's Handbook, 36th edition, David Lowe, 2005

The above titles are available from all good bookshops or direct from the publishers. To obtain more information, please contact the publisher at the address below:

Kogan Page
120 Pentonville Road
London N1 9JN
Tel: 020 7278 0433
Fax: 020 7837 6348
www.kogan-page.co.uk

ALSO AVAILABLE FROM KOGAN PAGE

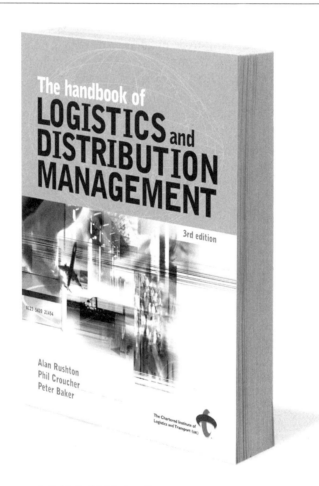

0 7494 4669 2   Paperback   2006

ALSO AVAILABLE FROM KOGAN PAGE

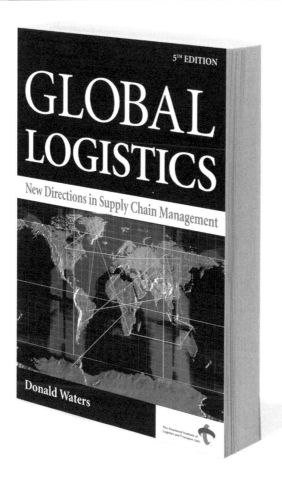

0 7494 4813 X   Paperback   2006